DIVINE BEAUTY, DIVINE GLORY

DIVINE BEAUTY, DIVINE GLORY

Knowing WHO God Is and Not Just What He DOES

Alison M. Down, MAPM

emerge
publishing

www.Emerge.pub

25 24 23 22 21 20   9 8 7 6 5 4 3 2 1

DIVINE BEAUTY DIVINE GLORY: KNOWING WHO GOD IS NOT JUST WHAT HE DOES
Copyright ©2020 Alison M. Down, MAPM

Published by:
Emerge Publishing, LLC • 9521 Riverside Parkway, Suite 243 Tulsa, OK 74137
Phone: 888.407.4447 • www.EmergePublishing.com

Library of Congress Cataloging-in-Publication Data:
ISBN: 978-1-949758-83-2 Paperback

BISAC:
REL012120   RELIGION / Christian Living / Spiritual Growth
REL067000   RELIGION / Christian Theology / General

Printed in the United States

CONTENTS

INTRODUCTION

THE BEAUTY AND THE GLORY OF THE DIVINE

"God is Love." So says 1 John 4:8, "God is love." This was the first sentence as well as the last sentence in the *Conflict of the Ages* series written by Ellen G. White. The question of interest is "What is love?" Who is this God who is *love*? How do we discover this God who is love?

The first song I sang in public was entitled "The Love of God":

> "The Love of God is greater far
> Than tongue or pen can ever tell
> It goes beyond the highest star
> And reaches to the lowest hell."

The book of Exodus provides us with a peek into the beauty and the glory of the Divine. It is often said God interweaves Himself in the affairs of man. He created humans and desires a relationship with us. His love for His creation is what draws us to Him. Moses was one who sought out God, who wanted to see the "glory" of God. God granted him his request, yet all the while protecting him, allowing him to see a glimpse of His Divine Glory. Moses' response? He worshiped this mighty God in whom he was developing a close, intimate relationship.

Jesus shared with three of His disciples in Matthew 17:1–8, Mark

9:2–8, Luke 9:28–36 a little of His own glory while on the Mount of Transfiguration. Is it possible that the pre-incarnate Second Person of the Godhead is the God of the burning bush? Is it likely the God on Mount Sinai was Jesus Himself in His Divine form? Can we surmise that the God who guided Moses and Aaron in their dealings with Pharaoh was Jesus who worked with a group of men and women, teaching them the art of discipling and preparing them to go into all the world *"baptizing them in the name of the Father and of the Son and of the Holy Spirit, teaching them to observe all that I have commanded you"* (Matt. 28:19–20 NASB).[1]

We will encounter divine holiness, experience divine power and embrace divine authority and divine grace. We will be compelled to recognize divine ownership and Divine Order. We will find divine mercy intertwining with divine justice, while divine presence and divine healing will demonstrate divine sustenance and divine action. As we consider all these attributes of this divine God, we will come to have a better understanding of WHO God is not just what He does. This God who created mankind as the climax of His creation, infused His love into Adam and Eve and subsequently into each one of us.

Thus, a study of the book of Exodus will provide the student of Scripture with ample opportunity to observe these and other divine attributes of the Creator/Redeemer God we are thrilled, excited, and exhilarated to worship. Examining, investigating, considering the words of the book of Exodus will also offer the possibility of developing a similar close, cherished, comfortable relationship with God Himself; this God whom we desire to adore and reverence because of who He is and not just what He can and does for us.

Are you ready to explore this amazing book with me? Let us begin.

---

[1] Unless otherwise indicated all Scripture quotations come from the English Standard Version.

DIVINE HOLINESS

Exodus 3:5, *"Then he said, 'Do not come near; take your sandals off your feet, for the place on which you are standing is holy ground.'"*

Moses was confronted by a burning bush, a bush that did not burn. He heard his name called but was told not to draw near. He was told to take off his sandals, so he took off his sandals for the ground was holy. What wtas it that made the ground holy? Only ONE makes the ground holy. Only ONE makes anything and anyone holy. That ONE is not wholly man, but wholly GOD.

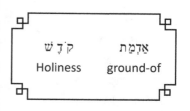

קֹ דֶ שׁ   אַדְמַת
Holiness   ground-of

The priests were not to enter the wilderness sanctuary with shoes upon their feet. Particles of dust clinging to them would desecrate the holy place. They were to leave their sandals in the courtyard before entering the sanctuary. They were commanded to wash both their hands and their feet before ministering in the tabernacle. God's presence in the wilderness tabernacle rendered it holy. Obedience, therefore, is a criterion for someone who wishes to enter God's presence.

Preparing to Meet God

Exodus 19:10–11, *"...the LORD said to Moses, 'Go to the people and consecrate them today and tomorrow and let them wash their garments and be ready for the third day. For on the third day the LORD will come down on Mount Sinai in the sight of all the people.'"*

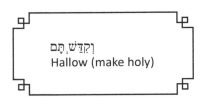

וְקִדַּשְׁתָּם

Hallow (make holy)

The Hebrew word for holy is found in the Hebrew word for consecrate. When God tells the Israelites to "be holy for I am holy (Lev. 20:26), He is revealing to them and subsequently to us today, that to be holy as He is holy means He must be within each one.

Preparation for the appearing of the LORD involves outward ritual preparation which reflects inner conviction. Note the importance of sacred space, as God dwells within so the individual becomes holy and consecrated and thus can enter God's presence as well. Hebrews 4:16 tells us to come boldly before the throne of grace. This is only possible when we consecrate ourselves and embrace the holiness of God. This will later become even more significant in the design of the tabernacle/temple. Because of the LORD's presence, a mountain became holy (vv. 12–13)

Thus, was constantly taught the lesson that all defilement must be put away from those who would approach the presence of God.[2]

Joshua on Holy Ground

Joshua 5:13–15, *"When Joshua was by Jericho, he lifted up his eyes and looked, and behold, a man was standing before him with his drawn sword in his hand. And Joshua went to him and said to him, 'Are you for us, or for our adversaries?' And he said, 'No; but I am the commander of the army of the LORD. Now I have come.' And Joshua fell on his face to the earth and worshiped and said to him, 'What does my lord say to his servant?' And the commander of the LORD's army said to Joshua, 'Take off*

---

[2] Ellen G. White, *Patriarchs and Prophets*, (Oshawa, ON: Signs of the Times Publishing Association, 1946), p. 350.

*your sandals from your feet, **for the place where you are stand-ing is holy.'** And Joshua did so."* (Emphasis mine.)

The man with the drawn sword was no ordinary man, but God Himself. Thus, the ground upon which Joshua was standing was considered holy. He called himself "commander of the Lord's army." The only other place where this same title is given is found in Daniel 8:11 translated as "Prince of the host."

Joshua asked the obvious question. God responded by saying "no," He was not the Commander **for** Israel; He was claiming to be Israel's Commander!

רַשׁ	הַצָּבָא
shr	tsba
chief-of	the-host

Joshua, as the new commander of Israel, was preparing himself and his people to enter Canaan. As he studied the plans, God appeared to him to reassure him in his task and to provide additional information for their preparations.

The inhabitants of Canaan had been granted ample opportunity for repentance. Forty years before, the opening of the Red Sea and the judgments upon Egypt had testified to the supreme power of the God of Israel. And now the overthrow of the kings of Midian, of Gilead, and Bashan had further shown that Jehovah was all gods. The holiness of His character and His abhorrence of impurity had been evidenced in the judgments visited upon Israel for their participation in the abominable rites of Baal Peor. All these events were known to the inhabitants of Jericho.[3]

The Sabbath – Holiness

The very first reference of holiness we find is in Genesis 2:2–3, *"And on the seventh day God **finished** his work that he had done, and he **rested** on the seventh day from all his work that*

וַיְשַׁבֹּת	וַיְכַל
and-he-is-ceasing	and-he-is-finishing
וַיְקַדֵּשׁ	וַיְבָרֶךְ
and-he-is-making-holy	and-he-is-blessing

[3] White, p. 492

*he had done. So God **blessed** the seventh day and made it **holy**, because on it, God rested from all his work that he had done in creation."* (Emphasis mine.)

We often look at this passage to PROVE the Sabbath is not a Jewish Commandment. We forget with who we are dealing. It states God finished, God rested, God blessed, God made it HOLY. Why? Because He rested. Whenever, however, wherever God rests, it is holy.

Consider the burning bush. Consider Joshua's confrontation with the Commander of the army of the Lord. Consider Nicodemus talking with Jesus. Consider the Samaritan woman at the well.

Yes, we must consider Jesus meeting us where we are, but we must also recognize a change is taking place. Unless we respond to that change, we will have negated the holiness of that time with God.

As the Israelites, for three days, were to consecrate themselves—wash their clothes, bathe, put on their best apparel—before approaching the throne of God, so today, who are we to neglect our duty in preparing to meet Him each Sabbath.

The Israelites were camped around the base of the Sinai; later, they would camp around the wilderness tabernacle. Both were to be a place of holiness, because God was there. Where God dwells, it is holy. This place was to be a place where the worshiper could come to commune with the one worshiped—God.

God blessed the Sabbath and made it holy for two reasons:

He desires community, He enjoys companionship, He craves relationship.

He has taken ownership of this **one** day, He has reserved title of this **one** day, He has acquired possession of this **one** day. He enjoys sharing this day with His guests.

We make appointments to see the doctor, to see the lawyer, to meet a friend at the restaurant. It would never occur to us to change the date and time of these appointments without prior knowledge on both parties. Why do we think we can change the day of worship to the Holy God for another day of our choosing?

Who are we to dare state, "If we worship God one day a week, we will be fine"? Some call worshiping God on His Sabbath as legalism. Guess what? He **OWNS** this day.

We own a piece of property, we invite friends and neighbors to visit. Why?

We crave companionship

We own this property and want to share its beauty with our guests.

John 3:16 says, *"For God so loved the world, that He gave His only Son, that whoever believes in Him, should not perish but have eternal life."*

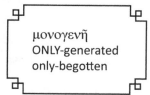

μονογενῆ
ONLY-generated
only-begotten

One and only—*monogenes*. Mono: unique, one of a kind. There are billions of humans living on earth today. There is only one God-Man alive today and His name is Jesus. Jesus is not just a big deal, He is *THE DEAL*.

He heals by His touch, He restores by His Word, He enjoys His handiwork, He reveals His character to His creation, He makes holy wherever He rests.

Revelation 4:10–11, *"the twenty-four elders fall down before Him who is seated on the throne and worship Him who lives forever and ever. They cast their crowns before the throne, saying, 'Worthy are you, our Lord and God, to receive glory and honor and power, for You created all things, and by Your will they were existed and were created."*

The twenty-four elders willingly surrender authority to the ONE worthy of worship. And why is this ONE to be worshiped? Because, He is Creator.

When Moses asked Him for His name, this was His response: *"I AM WHO I AM"* (Ex. 3:14). Another way to say this: "I AM WHAT I AM" or "I

WILL BE WHAT I WILL BE." Here, the God of the universe is resting within a burning bush. He carries on a conversation with His creation, allowing him (Moses) to ask Him questions, sharing with His child a little of His own presence.

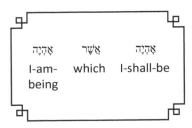

אֶהְיֶה	אֲשֶׁר	אֶהְיֶה
I-am-being	which	I-shall-be

God rested upon Mount Sinai and it became holy. God rested by the well and it became holy for the Samaritan woman. God rested while He presented the Sermon on the Mount and the people listening sense a change coming over them.

Jesus Resting on the Cross

The book entitled *The Desire of Ages* describes the tearing of the veil in the temple while Jesus is on the cross.

> "The earth trembles and quakes; for the Lord Himself draws near. With a rending noise the inner veil of the temple is torn from top to bottom by an unseen hand, throwing open to the gaze of the multitude a place **once filled with the presence of God**. [*Where was God? He was in the darkness surrounding His only Son on the cross. – Psalm 18:9–11.*] In this place the Shekinah had dwelt. Here God had manifested His glory above the mercy seat. [*Now, His glory is shrouded around His Son hanging on the cross.*] No one, but the high priest, ever lifted the veil separating this apartment from the rest of the temple. He entered in once a year to make an atonement for the sins of the people. But lo, this veil is rent in twain. The most holy place of the earthly sanctuary is no longer sacred. [*Why? Because the King of kings was hanging on a cross!*]"[4] (Emphasis mine.)

God rested on the cross and the history and the future of mankind changed. Jesus rested in the tomb, it could not hold Him. Morning arose,

---

[4] Ellen G. White, *The Desire of Ages*, (Oshawa, ON: Pacific Press Publishing Association, 2005), p. 757.

so did the Savior of the world. As He rose, He brought forth, besides His own glory, also the glory of the Father and the Spirit.

To understand God's holiness, we must draw near and rest near HIM. He is the Vine, we are the branches (Jn. 15:1–5). We must focus our attention upon HIM. There should be no other distraction which should be allowed to draw us away. As we approach Him, our voices will join the twenty-four elders in praising God and giving Him all glory and honor and power. Matthew 5:8, *"Blessed are the pure in heart, for they shall see God."* Jesus "meant far more than ceremonial or ritual purity and restraints against pollutants such as sensuality and lust. He was including all the desirable character traits and motives of the soul that is free from pride—that is not self-seeking, but is humble, unselfish, and childlike."[5]

What Is Holiness?

Man has attempted to define holiness as "in the highest sense belongs to God (Isaiah 6:3; Revelation 15:4), and to Christians as conse-crated to God's service, and in so far as they are conformed in all things to the will of God (Romans 6:19 Romans 6:22; Ephesians 1:4; Titus 1:8; 1 Peter 1:15). Personal holiness is a work of gradual development. It is carried on under many hindrances, hence the frequent admoni-tions to watchfulness, prayer, and perseverance (1 Corinthians 1:30; 2 [Corinthians] 7:1; Ephesians 4:23 Ephesians 4:24)"[6]

Shall we begin? Isaiah 6:3–5, *"And one called to another and said: 'Holy, holy, holy is the Lord of hosts; the whole earth is full of his glory!' And the foundations of the thresholds shook at the voice of him who called, and the house was filled with smoke. And I said: 'Woe is me! For I am lost; for I am a man of unclean lips, and I dwell in the midst*

---

[5] Hyveth Williams, *Secrets of a Happy Heart: A Fresh Look at the Sermon on the Mount,* (Hagerstown, MD: Review and Herald Publishing Association, 2004), p. 103.

[6] M.G. Easton MA, DD, *Illustrated Bible Dictionary, Third Edition,* (Nashville, TN: Thomas Nelson, 1897), Public Domain.

of a people of unclean lips; for my eyes have seen the King, the Lord of hosts!'"

The holiness of God illuminates the sinfulness of man.[7] The second beatitude in Matthew 5 talks of blessing those who mourn for they shall be comforted. The experience of the sinner who encounters this living and holy God brings out a mourning which expresses itself with tears and soul-searching silence.

Flowing from a conscience tenderly touched by the Holy Spirit, it mourns past sins and present unworthiness. Furthermore, such grief sympathizes with our Savior's sufferings—not once for all times, but, according to the verb's tense, a continuous experience.[8]

Revelation 1:7, *"Behold, he is coming with the clouds, and every eye will see him, even those who pierced him, and all tribes of the earth will wail [mourn] on account of him. Even so. Amen."* Why the mourning? Because "the holiness of God highlights our sins"[9]

Meeting God in His Holiness

Exodus 33:9, *"When Moses entered the tent [of meeting], the pillar of cloud would descend and stand at the entrance of the tent, and the Lord would speak with Moses."* The people watched Moses and they would worship afar off. They were terrified of confronting God themselves. They recognized "the holiness of God highlights the sin of man."[10]

---

[7] Max Lucado, *When God Whispers Your Name*, (Dallas, TX: Word Publishing, 1994), p. 182.

[8] Williams, p. 50

[9] Lucado, p. 182

[10] Ibid. p. 183

How was Moses able to meet with God? He was sinful as everyone else. He confronted God Himself. He approached God, seeking His holiness, desiring to become holy himself. God stated in Leviticus 11:44, 19:2, 20:7, *"You shall be holy, for I the Lord your God am holy."* Moses still wanted to see God's glory, in other words, God's holiness (Ex. 33:18).

God granted Moses' request, but He also protected Moses. Exodus 33:21–23, *"And the Lord said, 'Behold, there is a place by me where you shall stand on the rock, and while my glory passes by, I will put you in a cleft of the rock, and I will cover you with my hand until I have passed by. Then I will take away my hand, and you shall see my back, but my face shall not be seen.'"*

God described Himself as: *"'The Lord, the Lord, a God **merciful** and **gracious, slow to anger**, and **abounding in steadfast love** and **faithfulness**, keeping steadfast love for thousands **forgiving iniquity** and transgression and **sin**,*

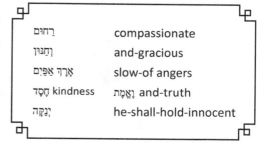

רַחוּם	compassionate
וְחַנּוּן	and-gracious
אֶרֶךְ אַפַּיִם	slow-of angers
חֶסֶד kindness	וֶאֱמֶת and-truth
יְנַקֶּה	he-shall-hold-innocent

*but who will by no means clear the guilty, visiting the iniquity of the fathers on the children and the children's children, to the third and the fourth generation.' **And Moses quickly bowed his head toward the earth and worshiped**"* (Ex. 34:6–8, emphasis mine).

Confronting the holiness of God causes one to worship.

Galatians 5:22–23 tells us, *"But the fruit of the Spirit is love, joy, peace, patience, kindness, goodness, faithfulness, gentleness, self-control; against such things there is no law."* Does this not describe God Himself? When we are imbued with these characteristics, we are taking on God's holiness, becoming more like Him as when He initially created our first parents.

Questions to Ponder:

Do I prepare myself to meet God?
What preparations do I make to meet God?
Have I sensed a change whenever I come into His presence?
Am I uplifting God's Name with my changed character?

Take Away Notes:

DIVINE WRATH DEMONSTRATES
DIVINE GRACE

Exodus 4:14–17 (NASB), *"Then the anger of the Lord burned against Moses, and He said, 'Is there not your brother Aaron the Levite? I know that he speaks fluently. And moreover, behold, he is coming out to meet you; when he sees you, he will be glad in his heart. You are to speak to him and put the words in his mouth; and I, even I, will be with your mouth and his mouth, and I will teach you what you are to do. Moreover, he shall speak for you to the people; and he will be as a mouth for you and you will be as God to him. You shall take in your hand this staff, with which you shall perform the signs.'"*

"This staff" will show up from time to time as God demonstrates His divine power and His divine authority.

Divine Anger and Punishment

Have you noticed there is not a word about punishment? Often, when anger erupts in humans, punishment or destruction follows on its heels. Not so with God. While Scripture reveals the trials and persecution by the various tribes around them in Canaan (see the book of Judges) and the ultimate captivity of Judah to Babylon, we must realize God's long-suffering attribute in other situations where His grace abounds. So, what do we do with the children of Israel (Num. 11:31–34), Balaam (Num. 22:22–35), Uzzah (2 Sam. 6:1–7; 1 Chron. 13:5–12), and Ananias and Sephirah (Acts 5:1–11)? How does God demonstrate His divine grace in these cases?

Case Studies

As we consider the motives, the actions, and the results in these cases, we will further understand and appreciate the divine wrath, all the while experiencing divine grace in each event, lessons which we would do well to fully understand.

(Ex.4:14) the anger of the Lord was **kindled;** (Yahweh יְהֹוָה; anger of אַף; and-he-is-being-hot וַיִּחַר) ;

(Num.11:33) the anger of the Lord was **kindled;** (Yahweh יְהֹוָה; and-anger-of וְאַף; he-was - hot חָרָה)

(Num. 22:22) but God's anger was **kindled;** (Elohim אֱלֹהִים; anger of אַף; and-he-is-being-hot וַיִּחַר)

(2 Sam. 6:7) the anger of the Lord was **kindled;** (Yahweh יְהֹוָה; anger of אַף; and-he-is-being-hot וַיִּחַר)

First, we must consider the use of the word "kindled." Three definitions are provided: "light or set on fire; arouse or inspire; be aroused."[11] This word suggests a beginning of anger as in starting a fire—the fire is small as it starts, and gradually gets bigger as it grows. There is some heat, but not enough to boil anything. In each of these cases, God's anger is "hot," suggesting more than just starting. Thus, the Hebrew word וַיִּחַר means something more than just being kindled. God's anger in these various stories suggests His anger was "hot"—He was very angry.

Yet in the previous chapter, we understood one element of God's holiness was "slow to anger." Yet we are now reviewing those times when God's anger was "and-he-is-being-hot."

---

[11] Lexico, "kindle" definition, The English Dictionary, accessed Feb. 8, 2020, https://www.lexico.com/en/definition/kindle.

Are we facing a discrepancy about God? As we consider these case histories, we may struggle to understand the wrath of God, how this wrath makes sense considering His own self-description. While the Word of God does demonstrate many logical life lessons, we must also realize the silence contains much teaching.

God's Divine Wrath

The wrath of God is seen most clearly against His Son on the cross, where Jesus carried the sins of the world. How did God treat the Sin-bearer? *God gave Him up.* God, the ultimate and only realist, allows natural consequences to run their course. Because freedom is sacred to God, He permits nature—even evil nature—to carry on. The worst thing and the best thing God can do to us is to let us have our way. After teaching us, disciplining us, warning us, pleading with us, and continuing to love us ("How can I give you up?" Hos. 11:8), God allows us to sleep in the beds we have made. [12]

Romans 1 explains further the divine wrath of God. Three times (verses 24, 26, and 28), God "gave them up." He allows us to make our own decision, to choose the course of action we wish, to determine for ourselves how we want to proceed; BUT, He also allows us to bear the consequences, reap the results, endure the outcomes from these choices.

When God withdraws His protecting hand, the forces of nature, the powers of darkness are taking over and forcing our submission. Ephesians 6:12 (NKJV), *"For we do not wrestle against flesh and blood, but against principalities, against powers, against the rulers of the darkness of this age, against spiritual hosts of wickedness in the heavenly places."* Thankfully, we do not need to fear these forces, these powers, because Jesus has gained the victory. But we still have our power of choice.

---

[12] Chris Blake, *Searching for a God to Love,* (Nampa, OH: Pacific Press Publishing, 1991) p. 202.

Reviewing the Stories

Israel's Sin (Num. 11): Gluttony, Ungratefulness

Israel has a history of complaining. No matter what God did, what Moses advised, what blessing or protection God placed upon them, it would appear that the only thing they knew was to complain. So, God gave them their desire.

God gave the people that which was not for their highest good because they persisted in desiring it; they would not be satisfied with those things that would prove a benefit to them. Their rebellious desires were gratified, but they were left to suffer the result.[13]

The people desired meat. They were used to eating the meat in Egypt and they wanted meat now. Verse 4 says, *"Now the rabble that was among them had a strong craving. And the people of Israel also wept again and said, 'Oh that we had meat to eat!'"* Who were the rabble? According to Exodus 12:38, they were "a mixed multitude" who exited Egypt at the time when the Israelites left Egypt. This mixed multitude incited the children of Israel to complain, especially about the manna God had so graciously been supplying to them.

People, generally, are complainers. We may have a roof over our heads, food on the table, a warm bed in which to sleep, all sorts of gadgets to lighten our load in life and yet we continue to complain. We are seldom satisfied with the bountiful gifts God provides to us. With all the blessings God provides to us, what are we lacking? His presence. But we cannot enter His presence as sinners.

In Numbers 11:18, we are told, *"And say to the people, 'Consecrate yourselves for tomorrow, and you shall eat meat, for you have wept in the hearing of the Lord, saying, "Who will give us meat to eat? For it was better for us in Egypt." Therefore, the Lord will give you meat, and you shall eat.'"*

---

[13] White, p. 382

Prior to receiving the Ten Commandments, the Israelites were instructed in preparing themselves to meet with God on the Mount. They knew what it meant to consecrate themselves now. The Lord brought the quail to a day's journey around the encampment.

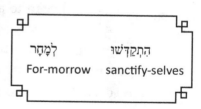

הִתְקַדָּשׁוּ	לְמָחָר
sanctify-selves	For-morrow

Regrettably, instead of preparing themselves, they rushed out and worked at collecting the quail not just for a few hours, but *"all that day, and all night and all the next day and gathered the quail"* (verse 32). Instead of consecrating themselves and giving thanks to God for this meat, their gluttony took over. Despising God, ignoring God's direction, being ungrateful for God's provision of manna, God disciplined more quickly than expected. The people who had yielded to their craving were killed and buried there.

But God's grace was present. Had God not destroyed those who through gluttony gathered the quail, this greed for self-indulgence, this cancer of covetousness would permeate even further throughout the encampment. We will see something similar in the case study of the early church of the New Testament.

Balaam (Num. 22–24): Greed, Stubbornness

This story of the talking donkey elicits several interesting points. Even while God is angry with Balaam for insisting upon going to Balak, despite the obvious sign provided to guide Balaam (22:20), God was still demonstrating His mercy.

Balak sent a delegation the first time, but Balaam following God's direction and refused to go with them. Balak sends a larger delegation, Balaam again tells them to wait until he heard from God. God had already spoken to Balaam, so why would he think God would change His mind? In a dream, God tells Balaam in Numbers 22:20:

*"**IF** the men have come to call you, rise, go with them."* IF introduces a conditional clause. Balaam knew God's direction, but he still dared to approach God to see if there was a change. (Some translations use the word "since," meaning "for the reason that; because.") God is allowing Balaam to choose the path he takes.

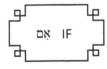

He did not seek to do the will of God, but chose his own course and then endeavored to secure the sanction of the Lord.[14]

> Psalm 81:11–12 tells us, *"But my people did not listen to my voice; Israel would not submit to me. So I gave them over to their stubborn hearts, to follow their own counsels."*

We still do this today. As children, how often we would pit one parent against the other in order to get what we were desiring? How often do we confront God Himself, hoping He will change His mind after He has answered our request, especially with a "no" response? We look at signs, omens, even a single word spoken in a timely fashion as a means of garnering our own desire. Thus, God gives us our own desires, but He also allows us to suffer the consequences.

Balaam knew Israel belonged to God. Still, he wanted material riches and he was willing to do anything to obtain those riches. Despite Balaam's desire to dabble in sin, aside from the fact Balaam's four oracles of blessing over the Israelites were uttered under the control of God, God continued to work and guide Balaam. Even the famous story of the talking donkey does not deter Balaam from the path he has chosen for himself. The mercy God showed Balaam demonstrates His great longing and love to each of us. This should encourage us to strive to follow God in all His leadings. Despite God's efforts to teach Balaam, to demonstrate to him the error of his ways, to validate His claim on Israel and thus on Balaam himself, Balaam met his end with the Midianites in

---

[14] White, *Patriarchs and Prophets*, p. 440

battle. All the riches, all the honor, all the prestige he garnered to himself could not save him in the end.

> "While they were under the divine protection, no people or nation, though aided by all the power of Satan, should be able to prevail against them…. And the favor of God at this time manifested toward Israel was to be an assurance of His protecting care for His obedient, faithful children in all ages. When Satan should inspire evil men to misrepresent, harass, and destroy God's people, this very occurrence would be brought to their remembrance, and would strengthen their courage and their faith in God."[15]

In Numbers 23:21, Balaam acknowledged *"The Lord their God is with them, and the shout of a king is among them."* The Hebrew word for "the shout of a king" is the same as found in Leviticus 23:24 and translated as "blowing of trumpets" to remind the people of God's pro-

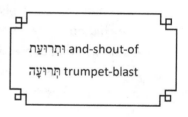

וּתְרוּעַת and-shout-of

תְּרוּעָה trumpet-blast

tection. By highlighting God's protection for His chosen people, because His presence is with them, God was mercifully warning Balak against hostile action.

Uzzah (2 Sam. 6:1–7; 1 Chron. 13:5–12): Presumption, Disrespect

> "The Israelites had in their hands a plain statement of the will of God in all these matters, and their neglect of these instructions was dishonoring to God. Upon Uzzah rested the greater guilt of presumption…. God can accept no partial obedience, no lax way of treating His commandments. By the judgment upon Uzzah He designed to impress upon all Israel the importance of giving strict heed to His requirements. Thus, the death of that one

---

[15] White, p. 449

man, by leading the people to repentance, might prevent the necessity of inflicting judgments upon thousands."[16]

Uzzah took it upon himself to handle the Ark. Was he a Levite of the family of Kohath? According to Numbers 4:15, *"And when Aaron and his sons have finished covering the sanctuary and all the furnishings of the sanctuary, as the camp sets out, after that the sons of Kohath shall come to carry these, but they must not touch the holy things, lest they die."*

The ark rested in Kiriath-Jearim, a community within Judah's territory. While David assembled all Israel, including the priests and Levites, there is no mention of Uzzah's clan. Aside from not knowing his lineage, the greater sin was the handling of the Ark. Instead of carrying the ark as God had earlier commanded, the ark was placed in a cart to be hauled by two oxen. The Philistines had sent the Ark back to Israel via a cart. They did not know better, but Israel did. Uzzah took the lead, and thus his sin was that of presumption. Could it be possible Uzzah took the lead because he was the owner of the place where the Ark rested? It does not matter whether Uzzah was the owner, he knew as did the rest of the Israelites, the Ark was to be carried upon the shoulders of specific people—the Kohath.

Again, God's mercy, God's grace is present. The whole group transporting the Ark knew better, yet not one stepped forward to encourage obedience to God's law, God's desire, God's command concerning the transporting of the Ark. It was the duty of the Kohath tribe to carry the Ark upon their shoulders, not placed in a cart. God has given us the responsibility of informing our brothers and sisters when, as a group, we are heading in the wrong direction.

As a young Pathfinder, my sister inadvertently turned on to a one-way street. She was leading the caravan of three cars on the way to a Pathfinder Camporee. She was now facing the oncoming traffic. The driver, the leader, in the car following continued along as well. He did

---

[16] Ibid., p. 706

not honk the horn in warning, nor did he flash his lights to get my sister's attention about the error she was about to make. Now there were two cars facing the oncoming traffic. My sister made the decision to stop. She spoke with a police officer who was nearby to determine the best way to get out of this situation. The leader said nothing, did nothing. He left her to decide the direction to take. His explanation? He did not want the group to get separated.

Uzzah took the leadership in this scenario, thus Uzzah received the punishment, therefore demonstrating to the remainder that God demands respect, God expects obedience, God is holy and so deserves reverence. Leadership has the added obligation to instill in the assembly; to encourage the congregation; to inspire the church, the dictates of the organization, the directives of policies and procedures, and ensure all is in accordance to the plain teachings of God.

While each one is considered a part of the priesthood, the leader—in this case, Uzzah—had the greater sin. He not only presumed to know, he rejected all that God had commanded.

Ananias and Sephirah (Acts 5:1–11): Greed, Deceit

How can we see God's mercy in this story? At first glance, it appears God took vengeance upon these two people. Looking a little deeper, we see two people who made a vow to God, received more than they expected, reneged on their vow, and then lied not just to Peter but more importantly to God, the Holy Spirit.

They regretted their vow, their hearts turned to stone; no more did they have joy in their hearts. When Ananias first arrived, he felt the guilt throbbing through his body, and when he heard Peter's pronouncement, he was overcome and fell dead at his feet. At least three hours went by and Sapphira arrived, carrying the same guilt as her husband, but now even more nervous, adding worry for her husband and anxiety as to what to expect. Seeing Peter, sensing in the silence of the people who were present, she knew all was not well. Enduring the questioning by Peter, she was overwhelmed when Peter told her of her grieving the Holy Spirit, she dropped dead.

> "Infinite Wisdom saw that this signal manifestation of the wrath of God was necessary to guard the young church from becoming demoralized.... This judgment testified that men cannot deceive God, that He detects the hidden sin of the heart, and that He will not be mocked. **It was designed as a warning to the church, to lead them to avoid pretense and hypocrisy, and to beware of robbing God.**"[17] (Emphasis mine.)

Jesus, Cleansing the Temple

Mark 11:15–18, *"And they came to Jerusalem. And he entered the temple and began to drive out those who sold and those who bought in the temple, and he overturned the tables of the money-changers and the seats of those who sold pigeons. And he would not allow anyone to carry anything through the temple. And he was teaching them and saying to them, 'Is it not written, "My house shall be called a house of prayer for all the nations"? But you have made it a den of robbers.' And the chief priests and the scribes heard it and were seeking a way to destroy him, for they feared him, because all the crowd was astonished at his teaching."*

In the time of Jesus' earthly ministry, the outer court designated for the Gentiles was being used to sell the various sacrificial animals and exchanging ordinary money into temple money. While one might consider this a good thing, especially for those who must travel a long way, this exercise became a blight, a means of extortion, an opportunity for a few to profit at the expense of their fellow worshipers.

---

[17] Ellen G. White, *The Acts of the Apostles*, (Mountain View, CA: Pacific Press Publishing Association, 1911), p. 73.

Two issues are of concern. Using the Gentile court for merchandise would eliminate the opportunity of the Gentile people to learn about the God of the Israelites. Selling the merchandise (sacrificial animals, temple money) for temple work could and would lead to extortion, overcharging, and mishandling of the funds meant for temple repairs, maintenance, and upkeep.

Final Destruction of the Wicked

Revelation 20:11–12, 15: *"Then I saw a great white throne and him who was seated on it. From his presence earth and sky fled away, and no place was found for them. And I saw the dead, great and small, standing before the throne, and books were opened. Then another book was opened, which is the book of life. And the dead were judged by what was written in the books, according to what they had done.... And if anyone's name was not found written in the book of life, he was thrown into the lake of fire."*

There is no eternal fiery hell, only a permanent separation from God. The wicked will be blotted from existence, no longer living, rather than enduring an endless punishment. God's mercy is demonstrated in this act.

So Why Did God Not Punish Moses?

"A man will gain power and efficiency as he accepts the responsibilities that God places upon him, and with his whole soul seeks to qualify himself to bear them aright.... The fact that a man feels his weakness is at least some evidence that he realizes the magnitude of the work appointed him, and that he will make God his counselor and his strength."[18]

---

[18] White, *Patriarchs and Prophets*, p. 255

This description of divine anger has nothing in common with human irrational rage, but further highlights divine grace. Throughout Scripture, we see the magnificence of God's anger demonstrating His awesome grace.

In each of these cases, God upholds His integrity, demonstrates His long-suffering love toward His creation, maintains His gracious handling of his errant children, and shows utmost mercy and goodness to each one. While He allows His children their choice, He also must allow them to experience the results of their choice.

Questions to Ponder:

Can I remember a time when I knew God should have been angry with me and yet I received His grace?

When I have been angry, have I shown this same grace to others as God has shown me?

Take Away Notes:

Divine Origin

Exodus 8:19 (NKJV), *"Then the magicians said to Pharaoh: 'This is the finger of God.' But Pharaoh's heart grew hard, and he did not heed them, just as the Lord had said."*

The magicians making this statement are not necessarily stating an expression of their faith, but rather a recognition of the originator of the plague. They have finally concluded this God was greater than themselves; and as the demons believe in God but tremble (Jas. 2:19), so also these people.

God has given us certain powers with which to carry out our daily activities, our life choices. But there is a limit to what we can and think we can do. It took to the third plague before the magicians conceded defeat. Rather than fight against God, it would behoove us to place our lives, our will in His will right from the beginning. But being human, we are tempted to take on more than we are able.

This was Lucifer's problem and this same thinking is what turned him into Satan. He refused to acknowledge the sovereignty of God. The day will come when even Satan will finally recognize, admit, and concede God is Sovereign. Isaiah 45:23, *"By myself I have sworn; from my mouth has gone out in righteousness a word that shall not return: 'To me **every knee shall bow, every tongue shall swear allegiance.'"*** Romans 14:11, *"As I live, says* the Lord, **every knee shall bow** to me, and **every tongue shall confess** to God." Philippians 2:10–11, "so that at the name of Jesus **every knee should bow,** in heaven and on earth and under the earth, and **every tongue confess** that Jesus Christ is Lord, to the glory of God the Father." (Emphasis mine.)

Every knee and every tongue mean not just human knees and tongues, but all creation, all angels, seraphim, creation of other worlds; all nature will bow in one accord before the Sovereign God of the whole universe and this includes Satan and his angels. What a day when that happens, to be a part of the throng who surround the King of kings and Lord of lords, praising His mighty power, giving Him the honor due to Him alone, acknowledging His glory.

The righteous will join with the angels and seraphim to sing!

Revelation 15:3–4, "And they sing the song of Moses, the servant of God, and the song of the Lamb, saying,

> 'Great and amazing are your deeds,
> O Lord God the Almighty!
> Just and true are your ways,
> O King of the nations!
> Who will not fear, O Lord,
> and glorify your name?
> For you alone are holy.
> All nations will come
> and worship you,
> for your righteous acts have been revealed.'"

The Finger of God

Exodus 31:18, "And he gave to Moses, when he had finished speaking with him on Mount Sinai, the two tablets of the testimony, tablets of stone, written with the finger of God."

God is the originator of the Ten Commandments, so who are we to think we can do whatever we wish with these Commandments? The first set of Commandments, God cut out the stone and wrote with His own finger the Commandments. The second set, Moses had to cut out two tablets and then God wrote the Commandments, again with His own finger.

Written on the Heart

When God created Adam and Eve, He placed within their hearts a knowledge of the law of God. They were acquainted with its claims upon them; they recognized the importance of the principles of God's authority, God's ownership, and God's Oneness. These precepts were written upon their hearts.

After their fall, Adam attempted to teach his descendants the law of God. This law was handed down from father to son through successive generations. Despite the gracious provision for man's redemption, few accepted it and rendered obedience. The law became perverted; as their hearts hardened, the law became cumbersome, unyielding to their degenerate thinking.

Abraham was given the rite of circumcision, a sign to demonstrate those who received it they were dedicated to the service of God. This sign would assist them to remain separate from idolatry and live in obedience to the law of God. This could be considered the first outward sign.

Moving to Egypt (during the famine at the time of Joseph), living amongst a nation of idolaters, subsequently being forced to submit enslavement to the Egyptians, these divine precepts became further corrupted with the revolting and prohibited teachings of heathenism.

God did not even then trust His precepts to the memory of a people who were prone to forget His requirements but wrote them upon tables of stone.[19]

---

[19] White, *Patriarchs and Prophets*, p. 364

Exodus 6:6–8, *"Say therefore to the people of Israel, 'I am the Lord, and **I will bring you out** from under the burdens of the Egyptians, and **I will deliver you** from slavery to them, and **I will redeem you** with an outstretched arm and with great acts of judgment. **I will take you** to be my people, and **I will be your God**, and you shall know that I am the Lord your God, who has brought you out from under the burdens of the Egyptians. **I will bring you into the land** that I swore to give to Abraham, to Isaac, and to Jacob. **I will give it to you** for a possession. I am the Lord."* (Emphasis mine.)

God is the originator of the covenant promise. He promised Abraham He would make him a great nation and in him *"all the families of the earth shall be blessed"* (Gen. 12:3 NKJV).

Seven times God says "I WILL":

וְהוֹצֵאתִי
And-I-bring-forth

"Bring you out" – We cannot in our own power leave the fleshly life of sin. We must depend upon God to "bring us out."

וְהִצַּלְתִּי
And-I-rescue

"Deliver you" – Only God can deliver us from the bondage of sin. Only God can rescue us from this life of sin.

וְגָאַלְתִּי
And-I-redeem

"Redeem you" – Through His own blood, He has redeemed us and made us free.

וְלָקַחְתִּי
And-I-take

"Take you" – "In the time of Jesus if a Jewish family lost all its wealth and prosperity, they could sell their freeborn children along with themselves into slavery. However, according to the Roman law, children who were formally slaves and then redeemed could not be sold again into slavery. To ensure this, they issued a document called the *exousia*, which functioned much as a legal certificate of adoption does today. The word also means legal right or authority—in this case, from God."[20]

"Be your God" – John 1:12–13, *"But to all who did receive him, who believed in his name, he gave the right [exousia] to become children of God, who were born, not of blood nor of the will of the flesh nor of the will of man, but of God."*

וְהָיִיתִי
And-I-become

"Bring you into" – Not only does He free us from our sinful habits, He will bring us to His home and make us His heirs.

וְהֵבֵאתִי
And-I-bring

"Give" – He died for our sins, but He rose again so He could give us a possession, a place in His new kingdom! (Jn. 14:1–3)

וְנָתַתִּי
And-I-give

The first three are promises of redemption and deliverance—bondage from sin and slavery to bad habits that affect our lives.

The next two are promises of adoption. We don't serve an impersonal God. God wants to be our Father. He desires above all to have a personal relationship with each of us.

The last two are promises of a new home and a new life—eternal life with new health, new strength, new mind, new heart.

One God, All of Me

Deuteronomy 6:4–7, *"Hear, O Israel: The Lord our God, the Lord is one. You shall love the Lord your God with all your heart and with all your soul and with all your might. And these words that*

---

[20] Williams, p. 121

I command you today shall be on your heart. You shall teach them diligently to your children and shall talk of them when you sit in your house, and when you walk by the way, and when you lie down, and when you rise."

The First Commandment states: *"You shall have no other gods before [beside] me"* (Ex. 20:3). God is God alone. There is to be no other. We are to worship ONE GOD. Not a thousand, not one another—only God. We are to give ALL our heart, our soul, and our might. Nothing is to be kept in reserve for ourselves.

When we give everything to God, He will provide everything we need or desire. When we place ourselves into His hands, we will not require more wealth, more possessions, more means. John 10:10, *"The thief comes only to steal and kill and destroy. I came that they may have life and have it abundantly."* This abundant life comprises of abounding fullness of joy and strength of mind, body, and soul. Who is this thief that comes to steal? Satan, straight and simple. He wants to destroy anything that has to do with God.

Ezekiel 11:19–20 (NIV), *"I will give them an undivided heart and put a new spirit in them; I will remove from them their heart of stone and give them a heart of flesh. Then they will follow my decrees and be careful to keep my laws. They will be my people, and I will be their God."*

According to the indigenous people, speaking in a dishonest way in order to deceive another is considered as "speaking with a forked tongue"—a divided heart.

Ezekiel 11:17–21 provides a summary of what will happen. God will restore His exiled people to their land, remove their idols, give them a new spirit, a heart of flesh, empower them to obey Him, and restore the covenant relationship with them. At the heart of this covenant is the relationship God wants with His own.

Ezekiel 36:26–27, *"And I will give you a new heart, and a new spirit I will put within you. And I will remove the heart of stone from your flesh and give you a heart of flesh. And I will put my Spirit within you and cause you to walk in my statutes and be careful to obey my rules [precepts]."*

We are talking about a heart transplant. God is willing to do this surgery, but the choice rests with us. Whenever we encounter God, there is always a place for change. When we do not see or experience a change, we have negated the holiness of time we have had with God. God meets us where we are, but there is always a change taking place.

"Obedience is not our achievement or performance, but a consequence of letting God work in us…. Power to overcome evil and live in harmony with His commandments comes from a source outside of us. Only the Spirit of God can transform hearts and enable people to observe His laws and instructions."[21]

Through the Holy Spirit, this law will be placed within the heart and mind of God's children, where it was always meant to be. Why? So that we might live in harmony with God's commands and belong to Him.

"Their God…My people" – covenant formula

Jeremiah 31:33–34, *"For this is the covenant that I will make with the house of Israel after those days, declares the Lord:* **I will put my law within them,** *and* **I will write it** *on their hearts. And* **I will be their God,** *and they shall be my people. And no longer shall each one teach his neighbor and each his brother, saying, 'Know the Lord,' for they shall all know me, from the least of them to*

---

[21] Andrews University Press, "Ezekiel 36:37," *Andrews Study Bible*, (Berrien Springs, MI: Andrews University Press).

*the greatest, declares the Lord. For **I will forgive** their iniquity, and **I will remember their sin no more.**"* (Emphasis mine.)

Through the Holy Spirit, God will place His laws within the hearts of His people, where it belongs and where it has always belonged. This is not referring to a New Covenant but the original covenant from the beginning, from Creation. Each of His people who enter this covenant relationship will not need teaching from others, but will receive instruction from God Himself. Why is this? Because each will love and obey God freely.

Hebrews 10:16 (NIV), *"This is the covenant I will make with them after that time, says the Lord. I will put my laws in their hearts, and I will write them on their minds."*

Hebrews 8:10 (NIV), *"This is the covenant I will establish with the people of Israel after that time, declares the Lord. I will put my laws in their minds and write them on their hearts. I will be their God, and they will be my people."*

The "New Covenant" experience does not exist apart from God's law, but is intimately connected to it (Matt. 22:36–40; Rom. 13:8–10; 2 Cor. 3:3, 6).[22]

"When God's love is responded to with faith, it produces a new covenant experience, which results in loving obedience. But if God is responded to with legalistic obedience (or with no obedience), it results in an old covenant experience. That's the significance of the old and new covenants in summary."[23]

---

[22] Andrews Study Bible, "Hebrews 8:10"

[23] Skip McCarty, *In Granite or Ingrained? What the Old and New Covenants Reveal about the Gospel, the Law, and the Sabbath*, (Berrien Springs, MI: Andrews University Press, 2007) Kindle Edition.

The "New" Covenant is the "Old" Covenant restated. Or should we say, these covenants are the original covenant God planned from the foundation of the world—Creation.

Questions to Ponder:

What is my relationship with God today?

If God were to ask me, "Where are you?" How would I respond?

Have I observed a change in my life since coming to know who God is?

Take Away Notes:

Divine Order and Action

G od is a God of order. Before He takes any action, He plans out everything beforehand. Unlike His children, God knows the end from the beginning because He is GOD! Thus, in the book of Exodus, we find this God, the God of Divine Order and divine action.

Before God did anything, He spoke to Moses and told him what to say and do. In the chapter "Divine Origin," God spells out what He would do for Israel, and subsequently, what He will do for us today. (Exodus 6:6–8, *"Say therefore to the people of Israel, 'I am the Lord, and I will bring you out from under the burdens of the Egyptians, and I will deliver you from slavery to them, and I will redeem you with an outstretched arm and with great acts of judgment. I will take you to be my people, and I will be your God, and you shall know that I am the Lord your God, who has brought you out from under the burdens of the Egyptians. I will bring you into the land that I swore to give to Abraham, to Isaac, and to Jacob. I will give it to you for a possession. I am the Lord.'"* [Emphasis mine.]) Step by step, God tells Moses all **HE** is going to do! None of these actions are carried out by Moses nor the children of Israel. Neither are we today responsible for any of these feats. None have the ability nor the power to carry these acts out.

Before each plague, God spoke to Moses in Exodus 7:2, *"You shall speak all I command you, and your brother Aaron shall tell Pharaoh to let the people go out of his land."* Here is an example of Divine Order:

The order of transmission is

God ⟶ Moses ⟶ Aaron ⟶ Pharaoh

Just because you are reading these words, or listening to my voice speaking to you, doesn't mean you are NOT hearing from God. If I, the messenger, have placed myself within the will of God, then you can safely be assured God is speaking to you. Therein lies the difficulty. That is why God gave us the gift of discernment, the ability to use the minds He placed within each one to be sensitive, selective, and discriminate.

There have been times when I have been speaking in a public place and suddenly realize the words God placed within my mouth to share with the listener(s) were words for myself to hear. When we worship God, God is the audience. When God speaks, we are the audience.

Plagues

God sent ten plagues that afflicted Egypt. As we review these plagues, we will also begin to recognize some of the attributes of God in laying these plagues upon the Egyptians and demonstrating some of His characteristics to His people, the Israelites.

First Plague: Water to Blood

Exodus 7:15–16, *"Go to Pharaoh in the morning, as he is going out to the water. Stand on the bank of the Nile to meet him and take in your hand the staff that turned into a serpent. And you shall say to him, 'The Lord, the God of the Hebrews, sent me to you, saying, "Let my people go, that they may serve me in the wilderness." But so far, you have not obeyed.'"*

Moses did as God ordered. Imagine Pharaoh heading out to the Nile to have his daily bathing ritual being confronted by Moses who told him God's message. His bath water turning to blood would be repulsive, but

He summoned his magicians and they appeared to have changed the water into blood as well. Even when the water life died, Pharaoh ignored the words of Moses. God did not speak directly to Pharaoh. He could have, but He is a God of Divine Order.

The Egyptians considered the Nile River to be the life source of their Pharaoh and hence themselves. Even with the water creatures dying in the bloody water, the attribute God is demonstrating to Pharaoh—God is LIFE.

Second Plague: Frogs

Seven days after the Nile had turned into blood, God said to Moses, *"Then the Lord said to Moses, 'Go in to and say to him, "Thus says the Lord, 'Let my people go, that they may serve me'"* (Ex. 8:1).

In the first plague, we have God calling Himself "the God of the Hebrews." In the second plague, He is calling them "His people." God is letting Pharaoh know His people belong to Him, not Pharaoh. He is stating His people are to serve God, not Pharaoh.

Moses warns Pharaoh that frogs will infest Egypt unless he obeys God. Exodus 8:5, *"And the Lord said to Moses, 'Say to Aaron, stretch out your hand with your staff....'"* Out from the Nile come the frogs. (The water creatures would have died in the bloody water, thus God demonstrates He is LIFE.) But the Egyptian magicians were also able to bring out the frogs.

Note the order of communication:
God ⟶ Moses ⟶ Aaron ⟶ Pharaoh

Pharaoh contacts Moses to have him plea with God to remove the frogs. Two interesting items come to the fore.

One: If the magicians were able to bring forth frogs, then why did Pharaoh not ask them to remove the frogs? The Bible does not tell us, but it appears likely he may have ordered his magicians to remove the frogs but they were not able to do so.

Two: Moses gave Pharaoh the choice of which day to remove these frogs. Pharaoh chose the next day, demonstrating that even in the minutiae, God interweaves Himself in our daily activities. This is more than the Israelites enjoyed. They had no choice, they had been dehumanized (made into slaves to serve the Egyptians); and by this time, they are demoralized. They basically have given up.

The Egyptians worshiped the frogs as their creator god. Since God produced frogs in such numbers as to overwhelm the Egyptians, they were forced to concede their frogs were not the creators, God is.

God is LIFE, God is CREATOR.

Third Plague: Gnats/Ticks/Lice

Exodus 8:16, *"Then the Lord said to Moses, 'Say to Aaron, "Stretch out your staff and strike the dust of the earth..."'"*

It would appear for this plague, Moses and Aaron are bypassing the Pharaoh. When the magicians again attempt to match Moses in producing the gnats, they find themselves powerless. They must concede, *"This is the finger of God"* (Ex. 8:19). Acknowledgement, yes; statement of faith, no.

Step by step, God is destroying, de-creating Egypt: first the water, then the earth, the animals, the people, the produce of the earth, total darkness, and finally death.

The Egyptians considered the gnats/ticks/lice capable of resurrection, especially for their Pharaoh. One by one and step by step, God is revealing His own characteristics not only to the Egyptians but also to the Israelites. Up to this time, the children of Israel were having to endure these plagues. These plagues were life lessons not just for the Egyptians but also for the Israelites.

God is LIFE, God is CREATOR. God alone is the RESURRECTION.

Fourth Plague: Flies

Exodus 8:20, *"Then the LORD said to Moses, 'Rise up early in the morning and present yourself to Pharaoh, as he goes out to the water, and say to him, "Thus says the LORD, 'Let my people go, that they may serve me.'"*

From now on, God separates His people from the Egyptians, thus presenting another demonstration—God is GOD; God is greater than any gods the Egyptians might worship. God is revealing to the children of Israel His concern, His love, His power.

Flies are extremity dirty, especially bearing in mind the dead fish (first plague) and dead frogs (second plague). Having to endure the stench of death, the Egyptians now must deal with pesky flies.

God is LIFE, God is CREATOR. God is the RESURRECTION. God is our PROTECTOR.

Fifth Plague: Death of Livestock

Exodus 9:1, *"Then the Lord said to Moses, 'Go in to Pharaoh and say to him, "Thus say the Lord, the God of the Hebrews, 'Let my people go, that they may serve me.'"*

As with the fourth plague, Moses warns Pharaoh that if he does not listen to God's voice, the plague will fall upon Egypt. The livelihood of the Egyptians is now being attacked. Today, it is our "pocketbook"; our bank account, when attacked, receives our utmost attention.

Again, God made a distinction between the Egyptians and His own people, as their own livestock remained untouched. Slowly, the children of Israel are beginning to place a little trust in this God of their fathers. Place yourself into their shoes. For six generations, they have been living in Egypt. (See the genealogy listed in Matthew 1: Abraham – Isaac – Jacob (goes to Egypt with his family of seventy) – Judah – Perez – Hezron – Ram – Amminadah – Nahshon. [Numbers 1:7 has Nahshon listed].) While they remember and continue to worship the God of their fathers, Abraham, Isaac, and Jacob, in some ways, they have been compromising their beliefs and embracing the theology of the Egyptians, because they are now serving the Egyptians as slaves for at least two of those generations.

God is LIFE, God is CREATOR. God is the RESURRECTION. God is our PROTECTOR. God is our SURETY.

Sixth Plague: Boils

Exodus 9:8, *"And the Lord said to Moses and Aaron, 'Take handfuls of soot from the kiln, and let Moses throw them in the air in sight of Pharaoh.'"*

This plague affected the health and the life of the people themselves. While the spreading of ashes for the Egyptians was a means of ending illness or epidemic, God used this to add to their wretchedness. It must be remembered this is a battle between the mighty Pharaoh, who considered himself a god to his people, and GOD Himself. As God had to deal with Lucifer in heaven (Rev. 12:7–8), so He is dealing with Pharaoh.

Once again, the Israelites were not affected, though they observe the results of this and the remaining plagues. This time, it is Moses who is to handle the task. God is stepping up the intensity of the plagues. God sometimes steps up the intensity, especially when we, today, are stubborn or are stiff-necked about the direction we are taking.

God is LIFE, God is CREATOR. God is the RESURRECTION. God is our PROTECTOR. God is our SURETY. God sustains our HEALTH.

Seventh Plague: Hail

Exodus 9:13, *"Then the LORD said to Moses, 'Rise up early in the morning and present yourself before Pharaoh say to him, "Thus says the LORD, the God of the Hebrews, 'Let my people go, that they may serve me.'"*

As with previous plagues:

Early in the morning – Do not wait until later in the day. Do not delay the activity till a future time. Do not postpone what can be done NOW.

Present yourself to Pharaoh – Meet Pharaoh on his turf. Seek an audience with the man himself. Place yourself in His path, in his place, his position.

With your staff in hand – Be ready for action, be ready to speak the words with conviction, be sure of your position; use the words, the actions, the gifts God provides.

Step by Step

God provides His direction to us today—step by step. Sometimes we may have to run to keep up with Him, sometimes we may walk side by side, but He will always direct our steps one step at a time. Our job is to place ourselves as close as possible to the side of God; rely upon His grace, His mercy, His power; being mindful we do not hold anything within ourselves to fight the battle(s); ever alert for the dictates from God as to our next action(s); and relying completely upon our Creator/ Redeemer, we will prevail and win the day.

The Egyptians considered weather elements as various types of judgments, especially hail. The hail, lightning, and fire God used demonstrated His control and His judgment over the deities of the Egyptians.

> God is LIFE, God is CREATOR. God is the RESURRECTION. God is our PROTECTOR. God is our SURETY. God sustains our HEALTH. God is our JUDGE.

Eighth Plague: Locusts

Exodus 10:2 explains the purpose of these plagues: *"and that you may tell in the hearing of your son and of your grandson how I have dealt harshly with the Egyptians and what signs I have done among them, that you may know I am the Lord."*

This was the problem from the very beginning of this book. Exodus 5:2 states, *"But Pharaoh said, 'Who is the Lord, that I should obey His voice and let Israel go?'"* Knowing God is more than intellectual knowledge, it is a relational, interpersonal, interactive knowledge, and a commitment to this relationship, this association.

Even Pharaoh's servants began to plead with him about letting the Israelites leave. They recognized Egypt was already ruined, so how could he not see it? Pharaoh now considers letting a few people leave, the men only, but Moses and Aaron declared they would need their whole families and all the animals to go. This was NOT acceptable to Pharaoh.

With the hail, death of the animals, their own frail health to maintain and restore, the locusts now would decimate the future crop, thus food for the coming days, for the Egyptians.

> God is LIFE, God is CREATOR. God is the RESURRECTION. God is our PROTECTOR. God is our SURETY. God sustains our HEALTH. God is our JUDGE. God gives us ABUNDANT LIFE.

Ninth Plague: Darkness

Exodus 10:21, *"Then the Lord said to Moses, 'Stretch out your hand toward heaven, that there may be darkness over the land of Egypt, **a darkness to be felt.'"*** (Emphasis mine.) This was not an ordinary darkness. A blackness in which the clamminess, the darkness, the airlessness could be sensed, experienced; a heaviness which gave cause for thought—"Who is this God who declares His sovereignty, His majesty, His ownership, His claim over the people whom Pharaoh considered his own property?"

This darkness was essentially the last chance the Egyptians would be given to turn their lives around. Without God, all is darkness; without God there is no light of knowledge, no Son-like companionship, no joy of life, no love of God.

What were the children of Israel thinking as they observed these plagues? Were they beginning to think for themselves— "God is all-powerful?" "God is true?" "God is sure?" "God is absolute?" "Can we truly trust this God of Creation?"

Pharaoh considered himself to be the sun god Ra. When God exposed Pharaoh to the plague of darkness He demonstrated and He revealed to Pharaoh himself his own helplessness against the mighty God of the universe.

God is LIFE, God is CREATOR. God is the RESURRECTION. God is our PROTECTOR. God is our SURETY. God sustains our HEALTH. God is our JUDGE. God gives us ABUNDANT LIFE. God is our LIGHT.

Tenth Plague: Death of the Firstborn

Exodus 11:1, *"And the Lord said to Moses, 'I will bring one more plague on Pharaoh and on Egypt. Afterward he will let you go from here. When he lets you go, he will surely drive you out of here altogether.'"*

This is the first and only plague in which God just tells Moses what is going to happen. No more does God have Moses confront Pharaoh; no more does He have Aaron stretch out his arm with his staff, nor pronounce words of the coming plague. This plague, God will handle Himself. This plague, God will carry out the judgment against Pharaoh and against Egypt.

Why this change in the order of communication? When a child requires punishment, the parent does not go to their neighbor to mete out the punishment. The parent carries it out himself. I recall my father telling me the punishment he was giving to me hurt him more than it would hurt me. Receiving the spanking, I did not believe him. But as a parent, it does hurt and hurts greatly when we must punish our own creation. Heart pain is much worse than physical pain.

God is LIFE, God is CREATOR. God is the RESURRECTION. God is our PROTECTOR. God is our SURETY. God sustains our HEALTH. God is our JUDGE. God gives us ABUNDANT LIFE. God is our LIGHT. God is GOD! Almighty GOD. Amazing GOD. Awesome GOD.

While these plagues occurred many, many years ago, we must review them from time to time; we must remind ourselves of God's power, that God is a God of Divine Order and action. Even during the time Jesus was on earth, He maintained Divine Order. There was nothing in His demeanor to indicate unplanned, unprepared, unintentional action. Everything He did was thought out ahead. How was He able to do this? He placed His will within the will of His Father. Through continuous communication with His heavenly Father, Jesus was able to accomplish the work assigned to Him.

Mark 4:37–40, *"a great windstorm arose, and the waves were breaking into the boat, so that the boat was already filling. But he was in the stern, asleep on the cushion. And they woke him and said to him, 'Teacher, do you not care that we are perishing?'*

And he awoke and rebuked the wind and said to the sea, 'Peace! Be still!' And the wind ceased, and there was a great calm. He said to them, 'Why are you so afraid? Have you still no faith?'" Jesus was able to sleep in the midst of the storm because His life was securely in the hands of His Father. This story is Jesus' demonstration we also can find the peace and rest if we would only place ourselves within the will of our God.

Even while the storm was raging around the disciples, the God of order had all in His control. Satan may attempt to give the impression he can bring about destruction, chaos, and storms in our lives, but if we would rely upon God's grace, we would find our lives becoming more stable and our foundation more solid.

God's Final Judgment

One more time will the God of the universe handle the final destruction of the wicked. Revelation 20:11–15 says, *"Then I saw a great white throne and him who was seated on it. From his presence earth and sky fled away, and no place was found for them. And I saw the dead, great and small, standing before the throne, and books were opened. Then another book was opened, which is the book of life. And the dead were judged by what was written in the books, according to what they had done. And the sea gave up the dead who were in it, Death and Hades gave up the dead who were in them, and they were judged, each one of them, according to what they had done. Then Death and Hades were thrown into the lake of fire. This is the second death, the lake of fire. And if anyone's name was not found written in the book of life, he was thrown into the lake of fire."*

Today, we must count the cost. Today, we must be willing to place our will within the will of God, so we might be able to complete the task God has given us. When we are securely in the hands of God, we have inner peace that only He can provide (Jn. 14:27). When we have peace with God, we can experience inner contentment.

Questions to ponder:

Am I willing to place my will within God's Will and go the distance with HIM to secure my place in heaven?

Have I seen God at work in my life and in the lives of my family and friends?

Do I trust God to take care of me, despite difficulties I might encounter?

Take Away Notes:

PART TWO:
DIVINE ORDER AND ACTION

God sent ten plagues that afflicted Egypt. During the review of these plagues, we have begun to recognize some of the attributes of God. God planned the whole thing out, not just for the benefit of the children of Israel, nor for the benefit of the Egyptians, but also for us today to understand who this God is. As He put into action His plan, He has demonstrated to all generations past and present His characteristics, His attributes, His qualities, His virtues, His assets.

We have come to realize God is LIFE, CREATOR, RESURRECTION, PROTECTOR, our SURETY. He sustains our HEALTH, He is our JUDGE, offers ABUNDANT LIFE, He is our LIGHT. God is GOD! He is Almighty GOD, amazing GOD, awesome GOD, all-powerful GOD, astounding GOD. And this God desires above all else to be our FATHER!

Moses' Task

While God took over the tenth plague, Moses was given the task of dealing with the children of Israel to prepare them for the departure. Not only were they to pack up their belongings for a major move, they were to plunder their neighbors, the Egyptians, of their gold, silver, and other valuables. On top of all that they were to prepare a special meal, which would be used in the coming years to help them remember this night.

Considering all that had taken place in the previous few weeks, one would wonder why God would institute this meal to be set apart from their daily routine, to be used as a reminder of their departure from Egypt. We celebrate today many holidays, birthdays, wedding anniversaries—why? To remind us of certain events which are important to us to remember. Which leads to another question of "why"— "Why is it important for us to remember something?"

When God created this earth in the beginning, He instituted the Sabbath to be used to remember that He, God, was the Creator. God knows from the beginning to the end. God knows us very well. God knows we will forget unless we have something to remember.

Jeremiah 31:34, *"For I will forgive their iniquity, and I will remember their sin no more."* Psalm 103:12, *"as far as the east is from the west, so far does he remove our transgressions from us."* God chooses to forget those sins we have confessed. He wants us to forget those sins as well. So why do we remember the hurts, the insults and yet forget the important things God wants us to remember?

Pharaoh had been given many chances to make his choice; the children of Israel, up to this point in time, were basically only onlookers. At the second plague of frogs, Pharaoh was given the choice of what day to have the frogs eliminated. Pharaoh was told to release the Israelites upon penalty of a given plague. Pharaoh refused in all plagues. By his actions, he demonstrated he had no concern even for his own people, the Egyptians. He did not care if they suffered. Pharaoh could be compared to Satan in this respect. Satan has no concern for anyone on earth. His only desire is to hurt God. By making God's creation suffer, he causes God to suffer. Throughout history, Satan has instigated various actions against God, against His WORD, and against His authority.

The Passover Ritual

While this last plague was ongoing, God instructed Moses in the Passover service. This Passover meal, ritual, service encompassed several elements.

All leaven was to be removed from their homes—they would not be taking any with them on their journey. Leaven associates with sin, and bread represents Jesus. Therefore, we could consider unleavened bread can also mean the sinless Savior, Jesus Christ. When we finally begin our journey to the heavenly home, we will not be carrying any leaven (sin) either.

The Passover lamb selected was to be without blemish, but sufficient for all members of the family partaking of the lamb without any of it left over. They were even instructed how to prepare the lamb for eating (roasted), also what they were to be wearing (traveling clothes and staff in hand) as they ate. Thus, they would be ready at a moment's notice when the cry sounded to move out.

The blood from the lamb was to be painted upon the doorposts and lintels of their homes.

During the next twenty-four hours, there would be much activity going on. Everyone was to be involved in the preparations. It would take each and every individual to pull this off. Today, we also must be fully engaged to complete the tasks God has given us, so we too can be ready at a moment's notice when Christ returns to make our journey to the heavenly kingdom. We are to love the Lord our God with all our hearts, all our souls, all our minds, and all our strength (Lk. 10:27). When we love Him this completely, we will want to obey His commands, His desire, and be ready to enter the conflict with His divine action plans.

God is a God of order. There are no short cuts, no incomplete actions, no inferior materials. Step by step, God completes the mission at hand.

Guidance

While in the wilderness, the children of Israel relied upon God not only to direct the route they were to take, but also when they were to travel.

Exodus 40:36–37, *"In all the travels of the Israelites, whenever the cloud lifted from above the tabernacle, they would set out; but if the cloud did not lift, they did not set out—until the day it lifted."* These verses also show us God's divine presence, which will be covered in depth later.

God also had a plan for providing the type and amount of food they would need while on their journey through the wilderness.

Exodus 16:4, *"Then the Lord said to Moses, 'Behold, I am about to rain bread from heaven for you, and the people shall go out and gather a day's portion every day, that I may test them, whether they will walk in my law or not.'"* For forty years, God provided their bread.

God planned out the route, the timing, the food, and even the method of travel. He demonstrated for forty years His Divine Order and His divine action.

Jesus' Work

Jesus healed many people during His time on earth. For each healing, He had a purpose and plan in mind. As we consider a couple of case studies, we will begin to understand even more just what an amazing God we serve.

The Blind Man

John 9:6–7 (KJV), *"When he had thus spoken, he spat on the ground, and made clay of the spittle, and he anointed the eyes of the blind man with the clay, and said unto him, Go, wash in the pool of Siloam, (which is by interpretation, Sent.) He went his way therefore, and washed, and came seeing."*

Blind Man: Spittle into dust – to make mud
(reminiscent of Christ's work as Creator)
Anointed blind man's eyes (Might Jesus have made the eyes?)
Told to wash in Pool of Siloam (the blind man also had a job to do)
Went and came back seeing – Why? Obedience

A Girl Restored to Life and a Woman Healed
(Matt. 9:18–26; Mk. 5:21–43; Lk. 8:40–56)

According to the Levitical law, touching a dead person or someone with a discharge, whether blood or otherwise, would make that individual unclean. In these stories, Jesus is dealing with both a dead girl and a lady with a bleeding disorder. Touch is important to Jesus.

He is also focusing upon two females: one a young insignificant child, and the other an older, beyond her prime woman. Neither would normally be considered valuable. Again, according to Levitical law (chapter 27), valuation of male and female was higher for males and lower for females.

The young girl needed an intercessor, her father, to intervene on her behalf. The woman had to break the law to be healed. Both required more than just a belief.

"To believe in Christ merely as the Saviour of the world can never bring healing to the soul. The faith that is unto salvation is not a mere assent to the truth of the gospel. True faith is that which receives Christ as a personal Saviour.... Many hold faith as an opinion. Saving faith is a transaction, by which those who receive Christ join themselves in covenant relation with God. A living faith means an increase of vigor, a confiding trust, by which, through the grace of Christ, the soul becomes a conquering power."[24]

Step by step, Jesus maintained Divine Order even while action was ongoing. Being approached by Jairus, the ruler of the synagogue, Jesus commenced walking with him to his home. Enroute, in the midst of a crowd, Jesus is touched by the woman. I wonder how many people this woman touched as she struggled through this crowd to touch the hem

---

[24] Ellen G. White, *The Ministry of Healing*, (Oshawa, ON: Pacific Press Publishing Association, 1942), p. 62.

of Jesus' robe? He stops, and the woman makes known her problem and subsequent wholeness—physically, mentally, and spiritually. Jesus proceeds onward to the girl. Touching her, He speaks life to her. Divine Order, divine action.

Creation: Genesis 1

LIGHT		
Atmosphere – Water		Land
Sun, Moon, Stars	Plants, Birds, and Fish	Animals and Man
SABBATH		

It took seven days to create this world. Yes, seven. While we contend God created the world in six days, it took the seventh day, for in this day, God shares His creation with His created beings. The work was not finished until the relationship aspect was initiated. Too often, we consider only the physical aspect to a human. To be human involves physical, mental, and spiritual aspects.

In medicine, an individual is not considered dead until there is no breath, no heartbeat, and no brain activity. Machines have been invented to aid breathing; medication has been introduced to keep the heart beating. There is a machine that determines brain activity, but nothing has been discovered to keep the brain active. Only God can do that.

The heart of the matter is the mental and spiritual center. It takes the brain to learn to love, it takes the mind to work out intricate computations and make decisions. It takes the heart and lungs functioning in order for the brain to function. God's order, God's action.

Psalm 127:1, *"Unless the Lord builds the house, the builders labor in vain. Unless the Lord watches over the city, the guards stand watch in vain."*

Without God, any effort we place into something is in vain. Too often, we jump into the fray and then wonder why things do not work out as we planned. We, too, need order before action.

> Luke 14:26–33, *"If anyone comes to Me and does not hate his father and mother, wife and children, brothers and sisters, yes, and his own life also, he cannot be My disciple. And whoever does not bear his cross and come after Me cannot be My disciple. For which of you, intending to build a tower, does not sit down first and count the cost, whether he has enough to finish it—lest, after he has laid the foundation, and is not able to finish, all who see it begin to mock him, saying, 'This man began to build and was not able to finish'? Or what king, going to make war against another king, does not sit down first and consider whether he is able with ten thousand to meet him who comes against him with twenty thousand? Or else, while the other is still a great way off, he sends a delegation and asks conditions of peace. So likewise, whoever of you does not forsake all that he has cannot be My disciple."*

Count the cost—consider all options—yea or nay. Whoever, whatever we might consider as being more important than God has become our god. God alone lays claim to our whole being (we are to love God with our all our mind, all our heart, all our strength), our time (God has set aside one-seventh of our time, in which we are to spend solely with Him, to remember He is our Creator), our possessions (God tests us whether we will trust Him to keep us as we return to Him one-tenth of our income).

Compliance – John Bunyan's Pilgrim's Progress

Compliance tended to go along with the popular opinion. This time, he decides he is going to go with Christian until he falls into the pond of despond. While he and Christian are wallowing in this pool, Compliance eventually makes it out of the pond—unfortunately, out on the wrong side. He does not care. He is thankful to be out at all. He did not count the cost of traveling with Christian on his pilgrim journey.

Divine Order leads to divine action.

Questions to Ponder:

Do I believe in God's plan for my life sufficiently enough to put my faith into action?

Is my living today demonstrating my trust in my heavenly Father?

Who am I focused upon as I go about my work, my play, my rest?

Take Away Notes:

DIVINE AUTHORITY

Exodus 8:22–23, *"But on that day **I will deal differently** with the land of Goshen, where my people live; no swarms of flies will be there, so that you will know that I, the Lord, am in this land. **I will make a distinction** between my people and your people. This sign will occur tomorrow."* (Emphasis mine.)

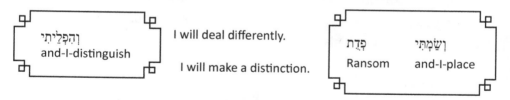

וְהִפְלֵיתִי
and-I-distinguish

I will deal differently.

I will make a distinction.

פְּדֻת   וְשַׂמְתִּי
Ransom   and-I-place

While God made a distinction/separation between the Israelites and the Egyptians, He was also introducing the element of ransom. The definition of ransom is: "a price paid for anything that has been forfeited."[25] The Israelites were slaves, but when they first came to Egypt, they were free men and women. Over the years, they forfeited their position of freedom. The ransom God was introducing would make them free again.

Scripture is as relevant today as when it was first written. Unless we study this book of authority, we will not understand the concepts God is wanting us to embrace. Today's society is demonstrating the results of

---

[25] "A Biblical and theological dictionary," Internet Archive, accessed February 9, 2020, https://archive.org/details/abiblicalandtheo00unknuoft/page/n425.

indifference, trusting in false precepts because people are ill-informed, illiterate, and ignorant about what is written in this Book.

John 8:34–36 says, *"Jesus answered them, 'Truly, truly, I say to you, everyone who practices sin is a slave to sin. The slave does not remain in the house forever; the son remains forever. So if the Son sets you free, you will be free indeed.'"* Jesus was speaking with the Pharisees who maintained they were already free, but did not understand and/or refused to accept the fact they were in bondage to sin, and it was Jesus Himself who would and could make them free if they would only accept.

When God made the distinction between the Egyptians and the Israelites, He was revealing to the Israelites they were no longer slaves— He was "redeeming" them. He was also informing the Egyptians they would not have continued control over the Israelites. Habits of sin are embedded in each one of us. We need the redeeming power of God to free us from these sins. God has the power, God has the ability and God has the authority to set us free. But we have been given the choice. Do we accept or do we reject Jesus' offer of ransom for our sins?

With the fourth plague (flies), God distinguished between Egypt and Israel. In several of the remaining plagues, this difference is explicitly demonstrated.

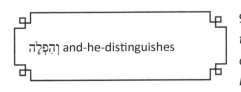

וְהִפְלָה and-he-distinguishes

Plague of Livestock's Death – Exodus 9:4 (NIV), *"But the Lord will make a distinction between the livestock of Israel and that of Egypt, so that no animal belonging to the Israelites will die."*

Plague of Boils – Exodus 9:11, *"And the magicians could not stand before Moses because of the boils, for the boils came upon the magicians and upon all the Egyptians."* (Implied.)

Plague of Hail – Exodus 9:26, *"Only in the land of Goshen, where the people of Israel were, was there no hail."*

Plague of Locusts – While there is no concrete reference to separating Israel from Egypt, we need to remember, the Israelites would not be harvesting the crop. Their slave days were almost at an end.

Plague of Darkness – Exodus 10:23 (NIV), *"No one could see anyone else or move about for three days. Yet all the Israelites had light in the places where they lived."*

Plague of Death of Firstborn – Exodus 11:7 (NIV), *"But among the Israelites not a dog will bark at any person or animal.' Then you will know that the Lord makes a distinction between Egypt and Israel."*

These verses should remind us today, God will and does make a distinction between His own and those who are against Him. As He separates us from those who refuse to choose Him and His gracious gift of redemption, we can gain assurance, He will stay by our side all the way.

Jesus Spoke with Authority

Mark 1:21–22, *"And they went into Capernaum, and immediately on the Sabbath he entered the synagogue and was teaching. And they were astonished at his teaching, for he taught them as one who had authority, and not as the scribes."*

While the scribes asserted themselves in their teaching, their words had no weight. They taught their own traditions—dealing *"mint and anise and cummin"* (Matt. 23:23)—as religion while ignoring *"judgment and mercy and faith."* Jesus' teaching was spiritual. He practiced what He preached.

God's Sign of Authority

What is the most obvious distinction that stands out to show the difference between God's people and Satan's people?

Matt. 13:24–30, *"He put another parable before them, saying, 'The kingdom of heaven may be compared to a man who sowed good seed in his field, but while his men were sleeping, his enemy came and sowed weeds among the wheat and went away. So when the plants came up and bore grain, then the weeds appeared also. And the servants of the master of the house came and said to him, "Master, did you not sow good seed in your field? How then does it have weeds?" He said to them, "An enemy has done this." So the servants said to him, "Then do you want us to go and gather them?" But he said, "No, lest in gathering the weeds you root up the wheat along with them. Let both grow together until the harvest, and at harvest time I will tell the reapers, 'Gather the weeds first and bind them in bundles to be burned but gather the wheat into my barn.'"*

This parable is unique to the book of Matthew, and it illustrates the mixed character of those in the church. Explicit is the warning that Christ's disciples should not anticipate the judgment by excluding members who are considered sinners. This parable rejects the strictures of the Pharisees and the Essenes that clearly separated the righteous and the unrighteous in their communities.[26] We will always find within the church, those who accept Jesus completely and unreservedly and those who speak the language but reject the Holy Spirit's leading. God knows who His true children are. He will reap the harvest when the time is ready, when the time is right, and when the time is fulfilled.

---

[26] Andrews Study Bible, NKJV, explanation of Matthew 13:24–30

Malachi 3:18, *"Then once more you shall see the distinction [discern] between the righteous and the wicked, between one who serves God and one who does not serve him."*

"Christ Himself will decide who are worthy to dwell with the family of heaven. He will judge every man according to His words and His works. Profession is as nothing in the scale. **It is character that decides destiny.**"[27] (Emphasis mine.)

I recently travelled north to visit some of the church members in Moosonee. I stayed at a bed and breakfast home. The hosts were very gracious, kind, and accommodating. There was one other guest present. This guest and I entered a conversation and found, to our delight and laughter, our differences. I thought she was a white person and she thought I was indigenous! We laughed heartily and enjoyed our time together in fellowship. We could not see a distinction in ourselves from the other. We were two women who happened to be in the same facility at the same time.

Distinction, difference, peculiar, these terms are often used to assist in determining some element or component of a people group. An obvious distinction known to mankind are the black people and white people. Despite this, each group further separates into subgroups. Of the black people, we have those from Africa, Caribbean and South Seas. The white people continue to have separate distinctions of those from Europe, North America, and again South Seas. This distinction is made only by man, not by God. Mankind was created by God. At the foot of the cross we are all equal, there is no distinction made by God.

What does God use to make a distinction? Or might a better question be: How does God demonstrate a distinction among His own "peculiar" people and those who refuse to be His own select people?

---

[27] Ellen G. White, *Christ's Object Lessons,* (Rocky Hill, CT: Review and Herald Publishing Association, 1941), p. 74.

Seal of God

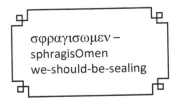

σφραγισωμεν –
sphragisOmen
we-should-be-sealing

Revelation 7:3, *"Do not harm the earth or the sea or the trees, until we have sealed the servants of our God on their foreheads."*

What Is This Seal?

Seal – Sign of God's ownership and authority (Rev. 9:4, 14:1; 2 Tim. 2:19)[28] Bearing the seal of God in the forehead demonstrates our character reflecting the character of God. The moon has no light, it reflects the sun's light. The still waters reflect the trees along its banks. The nearer the reflection is to the reflected, the clearer the reflection becomes. Thus, the closer we come to God, the more fully will we reflect His character.

The anguish and humiliation of God's people is unmistakable evidence that they are regaining the strength and nobility of character lost in consequence of sin. It is because they are drawing nearer to Christ, because their eyes are fixed on His perfect purity, that they discern so clearly the exceeding sinfulness of sin. Meekness and lowliness are the conditions of success and victory. A crown of glory awaits those who bow at the foot of the cross.[29]

The more clearly we discern the evils of sin, the less power Satan has over us. God's authority reigns within us, giving us the power to overthrow Satan's power. Satan becomes impotent.

Ezekiel 9:2–4, *"And behold, six men came from the direction of the upper gate, which faces north, each with his weapon for*

---

[28] Andrews Study Bible, Revelation 7:2. In the Hebrew context, name represents character. To have the name or seal on the forehead means to reflect God's character in life. Possible reference to the Sabbath (Rev. 13:16–17).

[29] Ellen G. White, *Prophets and Kings,* (Nampa, ID: Pacific Press Publishing Association, 1943), p. 590.

slaughter in his hand, and with them was a man clothed in linen, with a writing case at his waist. And they went in and stood beside the bronze altar. And the Lord said to him, 'Pass through the city, through Jerusalem, and put a mark on the foreheads of the men who sigh and groan over all the abominations that are committed in it.'"

In Hebrew, *"tau"* is the last letter of the alphabet. "It was a symbol of the last or remaining ones, faithful remnant ones, who 'sigh and cry' for the abomination done in Jerusalem."[30]

The Great Seal of Canada from King George V time. After his death, when his daughter became queen, the dye for making his seal was broken and a new dye was created in order to make the seal denoting Queen Elizabeth II as now the rightful ruler.

Components of a Seal

The Great Seal of Canada is used on all state documents such as proclamations and commissions of cabinet ministers, senators, judges, and senior government officials.

The seal dye is made of specially tempered steel, weighs 3.75 kilograms (8.27 pounds), and is 127 millimeters (five inches) in diameter. The image depicts the king enthroned on the coronation chair and robed, holding the orb and scepter, and the 1957 version of the Royal

---

[30] Andrews Study Bible, Ezekiel 9:4. It parallels the "seal of God" marked in the forehead (mind or character) of His end-time remnant. (Rev. 7:14)

Arms of Canada in front. Around the perimeter is inscribed *"REINE DU CANADA—ELIZABETH II—QUEEN OF CANADA."* Previous Great Seals of Canada were inscribed in Latin.[31] The seal dates back to the beginning of the reign of Elizabeth the Second, Queen of Canada. A new seal will be struck for her successor.

There are three elements in this seal:

The Name – Queen Elizabeth II

The Title – Queen of Canada

The Authority – Covers All Levels of Canadian Government

Does God have a seal? What does this seal or mark represent? Is there any place in Scripture where the elements of the seal of God is recorded? As indicated earlier, God does not want the earth destroyed until His people have been sealed. What then is His seal?

Seal of God

---

[31] "The Great Seal in the reign of King George V," image accessed February 9, 2020, https://commons.wikimedia.org/wiki/File:Great_Seal_of_Canada_-_King_George_V.jpg.

[32] Image, The Bible Sabbath, accessed March 7, 2020, http://thebiblesabbath.com/Sabbath-pres/sabbath-9.htm.

Exodus 20:8–11, "*Remember the Sabbath day, to keep it holy. 9 Six days you shall labor, and do all your work, but the seventh day is a Sabbath to **the Lord your God** [Name]. On it you shall not do any work, you, or your son, or your daughter, your male servant, or your female servant, or your livestock, or the sojourner who is within your gates. For in six days **the Lord made heaven and earth,** [Title – Creator] the sea, and all that is in them, and rested on the seventh day. Therefore, **the Lord blessed the Sabbath day and made it holy** [His Authority]."* (Emphasis mine.)

The Name – "The Lord They God"

The Title –The Creator of Heaven and Earth

The Authority – "The Lord blessed the Sabbath day and made it holy."

The Sabbath command, which is part of the Ten Commandments of God given to the Israelites, contain all three elements of a covenant seal. It appears logical then that Satan would present another day as his mark or ownership and authority.

The first time that Ellen G. White associated the seal of God with the Sabbath was in 1848. A few months later, in January 1849, Joseph Bates, the pioneer Sabbath theologian, published the first Adventist book on the subject and called it *A Seal of the Living God*. One of Ellen White's arguments that the seal of God is the Sabbath was that the Sabbath commandment contains the characteristics of a seal. A seal—she observed in our early days and reiterated many years later—is attached to a law to show the name, title, and authority of the lawgiver. The Sabbath commandment can therefore be considered a seal because it "is the only one of all the ten in which are found both the name and the title of the Lawgiver. It is the only one that shows by whose authority the law is given. Thus, it contains the seal of God, affixed to His law as evidence of its authenticity and binding force."[33]

Years of research, study, investigation has provided many books proving what the Bible is saying. Foundational to all study is the Word of God itself. The Bible explains itself to the ardent student. God will fill the minds of His people with His wisdom, as each continue to search deeply with the Holy Spirit's guidance.

Satan's Mark

On the other hand, Satan, who is opposing God and His authority, has his own mark.

Revelation 13:16–17, *"Also it causes all, both small and great, both rich and poor, both free and slave, to be marked on the right hand or the forehead, so that no one can buy or sell unless he has the mark, that is, the name of the beast or the number of its name."*

Satan counterfeits God's seal.

Mark of the Beast:

The Name – The beast receives it power, authority, and territory from Satan.

The Territory – Populated World

The Authority – The dragon, the Serpent, the Devil, Satan: he is destruction, chaos.

God is asking for people's loyalty and support, but He leaves all free to choose.

---

[33] White, Patriarchs and Prophets, p. 307

Satan also asks for people's loyalty, but once choice is made, it is extremely difficult to be released except through the blood of Christ.

The choice again is ours to make. Am I willing to place my will into God's hands? This is the question each one must ask themselves. When we do not ask this of ourselves, we have already made our decision, our choice, by default.

Questions to Ponder:

Do I accept divine authority enough to pay attention to God's message?

Am I willing to submit to the authority of God?

Take Away Notes:

DIVINE POWER

Exodus 9:16, *"But I have raised you up for this very purpose, that I might show you my power and that my name might be proclaimed in all the earth."*

Energy, vitality, force, strength, vivacity.

Through Moses, God told Pharaoh He wanted to demonstrate His power, so Pharaoh would acknowledge his own weakness. But Pharaoh was stubborn and refused to acknowledge this mighty and powerful God—the Creator.

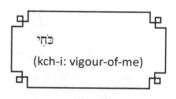

כֹּחִי

(kch-i: vigour-of-me)

God is a mighty God. God is a powerful God. But God is also a gentle God (a gentleman), a respectful God. God has given us the power of determination. God thus allows us to make our own choice, our own decisions. Therefore, we must acknowledge the outcome of our resolutions, and recognize our decisions will have an impact not only upon our lives, but also upon the lives of others around us. And this influence, this affect will shape not just the immediate moment of time but will have long-lasting consequences.

Hardening the Heart

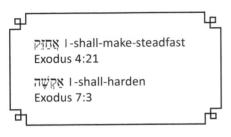

אֲחַזֵּק I-shall-make-steadfast
Exodus 4:21

אַקְשֶׁה I-shall-harden
Exodus 7:3

In Exodus 4:21, God states, *"but I will harden his heart"*; and in 7:3, *"I will harden Pharaoh's heart."* How do we reconcile this concept? Did Pharaoh not have a choice in the matter? When we study the Hebrew words, we note different words being translated as "hardened." Is there a difference in definition? Steadfast can be defined by using such words as unwavering, resolute, unswerving, firm, stubborn. Harden denotes toughening, coarsen, reinforcing, resistant, hard-edged, callused.

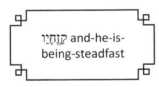

קַיֶּחֱזַק and-he-is-being-steadfast

First, we must recognize Pharaoh was not an innocent or godly man. He was a brutal dictator. After Aaron's rod had eaten the magicians' snakes, *"Pharaoh's heart was hardened"* (Ex. 7:13).

Second, Pharaoh hardened his own heart against letting the Israelites go, because his magicians were able to produce blood from water: *"Pharaoh's heart remained hardened...and he did not take even this to heart* (verse 22–23). Pharaoh heard no one—not God, not Moses, not even his own magicians, astrologers, spiritual counsellors. Pharaoh had his own mind set upon his individual course, his private desires, his own cravings. For the frogs, once they were gone, *"he hardened [הִקְשֶׁה] his heart"* (Ex. 8:15).

It could be that, as a result of Pharaoh's hard-heartedness, God hardened Pharaoh's heart even further, allowing for the last few plagues and bringing God's full glory into view (Ex. 9:12; 10:20, 27).[34]

Romans tells us we have "no excuse" not to know the secrets God shares with us. As we judge, so we demonstrate our own condemnation

---

[34] "Why did God harden Pharaoh's heart?" Got Questions, accessed February 9, 2020, https://www.gotquestions.org/God-harden-Pharaoh-heart.html.

(Rom. 1:20; 2:1). By refusing to acknowledge the sovereignty of God, rejecting God's honor, despising God's position as God Almighty, God's response is to "give us up" to our own delusions.

The disciples ran into this problem from time to time. In Mark 6, the story is told of Jesus walking on the water. The disciples are afraid, and Jesus reassures them. They did not understand because "their hearts were hardened". In Mark 16, Jesus rebukes His disciples because of their heart-hardness and unbelief.

"When hardness of heart is spoken of as a sin, the terms designate the committal of the will to a false position; a stubbornness in regard to the claims of God; an attitude of disobedience and self-will…. Whenever the heart is hard, there is unbelief; and this unbelief in regard to the love of Christ, this withholding confidence in this love, this refusing to yield the mind up to its influence, prevents this love from overcoming and subduing the mind."[35]

It should be noted, *"the LORD hardened (יְחַזֵּק) the heart of Pharaoh, and he did not listen to them"* (9:12). Boils were upon the Egyptians

---

[35] Charles G. Finney, "Hardness of Heart," The Gospel of Truth, March 16, 1861, accessed February 9, 2020, https://www.gospeltruth.net/1861OE/610313_hardness_heart.htm. Effects of hard-heartedness. Taken from 1861 sermon, "The Oberlin Evangelist" by Charles Finney.
1. A want of honesty and openness. 2. Prejudice – pre-judgment. 3. The absence of tender and kindly feeling. 4. Inability to appreciate the necessity of atonement; to honor God who has been dishonored by sin; and to honor the law that has been degraded by sin. 5. Slow to admit we deserve the punishment. 6. Devalue the compassion and forbearance of God. 7. Cheapen the love of Christ. 8. Does not appreciate the guilt that is involved in neglecting to labor for the souls of others. 9. God will be neglected; prayer will be neglected; praise will be neglected; obedience will be neglected; love will be withheld; confidence will be withheld; gratitude will be withheld; obedience from the heart will be withheld; and nothing will be present but cold formality and religious. 10. Uncharitable. 11. Self-justifying spirit. 12. Lack of conviction. 13. Self-deception, spiritual blindness. 14. Constant tendency to excuse all religious delinquency. 15. Selfishness. 16. Stinginess. 17. Superficiality in confessing. 18. Indulge in resentful feelings. 19. Lack of desire for spiritual prayer. 20. Total absence of a loving and compassionate spirit. 21. Reckless of their influence. 22. No true brotherly love.

including the magicians. Pharaoh was not even willing to listen to his own magicians—that is how hardened he had become.

Hard or Harsh

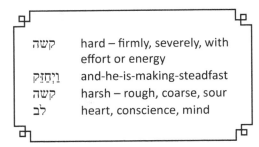

קָשָׁה	hard – firmly, severely, with effort or energy
וַיְחַזֵּק	and-he-is-making-steadfast
קָשֶׁה	harsh – rough, coarse, sour
לֵב	heart, conscience, mind

As we consider the translation possibilities, it comes to mind with the changing of word meanings over the years, today, we should consider God was saying He "will be harsh with Pharaoh's heart, will be rough with his conscience." This meaning today might make more sense than holding to the older translation words of God making someone's heart hard.

Sometimes, harshness is needed to prick through the conscience in order to reach the mind of the sinner's need for the Savior.

There was a time when parents would practice "tough love." This love was to make the child realize the error of his/her way. Parents, during this "tough love," were often in much prayer themselves as they dealt with their wayward child.

Using the plagues, God worked upon Pharaoh's heart, but Pharaoh was stubborn, stiff-necked, obstinate, inflexible, unwilling to yield what he considered his own position. He forgot God had placed him on the throne. He forgot God could and would easily remove him from the throne.

One thing we do know, God is a merciful God. While God is just in punishing Pharaoh, He did not utterly destroy Egypt. Egypt is present today, though not in the power it once enjoyed.

God Chooses

God has given man the power to decide for himself. The same holds true for God; He also has the power to decide. He provided within mankind the ability to reason, to formulate, to plan to determine a course of action. There is no other creature on earth who has been given this ability. All creation works on instinct, reflex, reaction to a given situation. They hold the "fight or flight" response to any immediate condition.

This is presented in Isaiah 1:18, *"Come now, let us reason together, says the Lord: though your sins are like scarlet, they shall be as white as snow; though they are red like crimson, they shall become like wool."* God desires communion, a relationship. He created man to be in His image, not just physically, but also mentally and spiritually.

Numbers 17:5, *"the staff of the man whom I choose shall sprout."* Leadership has always been a problem. When men attempt to control others because of their supposed position, they forget it was God who placed them in that position in the first place.

After the Korah, Abiram, and Dathan incident (Num. 16), the people of Israel still complained to Moses and Aaron, accusing them of killing holy people. God was going to destroy the whole community, but Moses and Aaron interceded on their behalf.

It is interesting to note, despite Korah, Abiram and Dathan being swallowed up by the earth, the people still complained, accusing Moses and Aaron of killing "holy" people. Earlier in Exodus 4, God told Moses the people would need signs to help their unbelief. While these signs demonstrated God's power, these signs also demonstrated God's authority.

Today, God still gives signs to assist us in making decisions. We are very slow to accept fully God's leading. We tend to bind ourselves to the teachings of our forebears, even when they did not have all the information.

Finally, we find in chapter 17 of Numbers, the story of the twelve rods, which represented each of the tribes. God presented an opportunity for the people to finally realize it is God Himself who chooses whom He will place in the hierarchy of the people. Each tribe was to bring a staff and write upon those staffs their tribe's name. These staffs were then placed in the tent of meeting. The next day, these rods were brought out. It was

Aaron's rod which bore the fruit. In this instance, this sign from God was intended to be a warning to the people, cautioning them to complain less, counseling them to accept the leadership God chose.

Only divine power could make a dried, dead rod not only come to life, but turn it into a fruitful branch. Only divine power can turn a dead ministry into a vibrant priestly ministry. Only divine power can revive a drug-induced, unyielding, semi-comatose mind; or revitalize a power-hungry, money-grabbing hypocrite, turning them into His own children, directing them to higher service for Him, pointing them in the direction of eternal life.

Mitch Albom shared in his book, *Have a Little Faith*, a conversation he had with his elderly Rabbi. It goes like this:

Do you think it's true—I asked the Reb that day—that our nature is evil?

"No," he said. "I believe there is goodness in man."

So we do have better angels?

"Deep down, yes."

Then why do we do so many bad things?

He sighed. "Because one thing God gave us—and I'm afraid it's at times a little too much—is free will. Freedom to choose. I believe He gave us everything we needed to build a beautiful world, if we choose wisely.

"But we can also choose badly. And we can mess things up something awful."

Can man change between good and evil?

The Reb nodded slowly. "In both directions."[36]

---

[36] Mitch Albom, *Have a Little Faith: A True Story,* (New York, NY: Hyperion, 2009), pg. 197

Choice is a powerful tool in the hand of man. Unless the individual has a relationship with the heavenly Father, the choices he makes can and does make for life and death decisions. While God chooses us to be His own, to become a part of His family, to be adopted into the heavenly realm, He allows us the choice to accept. It truly is a life and death decision.

Divine Power Within

Ephesians 3:14–21, *"For this reason I bow my knees before the Father, from whom every family in heaven and on earth is named, that according to the riches of his glory he may grant you to be strengthened with power through his Spirit in your inner being, so that Christ may dwell in your hearts through faith—that you, being rooted and grounded in love, may have strength to comprehend with all the saints what is the breadth and length and height and depth, and to know the love of Christ that surpasses knowledge, that you may be filled with all the fullness of God. Now to Him who is able to do far more abundantly than all that we ask or think, according to the power at work within us, to him be glory in the church and in Christ Jesus throughout all generations, forever and ever. Amen."*

Paul wrote this epistle while in prison. His parishioners are disheartened, discouraged, and dejected knowing of Paul's imprisonment. He wrote this letter to encourage them to stay the course and to recognize the power of God is still within each one. Divine power is possible as long as the Holy Spirit dwells within us. We may not understand this power, but if we accept the Holy Spirit's indwelling and allow the Holy Spirit freedom to work within us, He will produce the power we need, at the time we need it, and how much we need to face whatever trial or testing which comes before us.

"Truth in Christ and through Christ is measureless.... Not in this life shall we comprehend the mystery of God's love in giving His Son to be the propitiation for our sins.... The truth as it is in Jesus can be experienced, but never explained. Its height and breadth and depth pass our knowledge. We may task our imagination to the utmost, and then we shall see only dimly the outlines of a love that is unexplainable, that is as high as heaven, but that stooped to the earth to stamp the image of God on all mankind."[37]

Jesus told us in John 15:5, *"without Me you can do nothing."* Paul also stresses in Philippians 4:13, *"I can do all things through Christ who strengthens me."*

"Abiding in Christ means a constant receiving of His Spirit, a life of **unreserved surrender** to His service. The channel of **communication must be open continually** between man and his God.[38] (Emphasis mine.)

There can be no holding back a portion for ourselves, we must surrender fully and completely. Unless we have continuous communication, how can we hope to access the power of God to uphold us to His glory, to fill us with His influence, directing us with His sovereignty?

Jehoshaphat's Position

Chronicles 20:3, 6, 12: *"Then Jehoshaphat was afraid and set his face to seek the Lord.... And Jehoshaphat stood in the assembly of Judah and Jerusalem, in the house of the LORD before the new court and said, 'O LORD God of our fathers, are you not God in heaven? You rule over all the kingdoms of the nations. In your*

[37] White, *Christ's Object Lessons,* p. 128

[38] White, The Desire of Ages, p. 676

*hand are power and might, so that none is able to withstand
you....' O our God, will you not execute judgment on them? For
we are powerless against this great horde that is coming against
us. We do not know what to do, but our eyes are on you."*

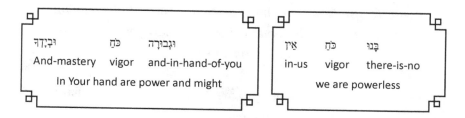

Jehoshaphat, king of Judah, recognized his need of God's power. He
prepared his armies, supplying them with the tools they would need
and the exercises to handle these tools. He stocked the city with food,
provisions, and the necessities to live while barricaded within the walls.
He ensured the water supply was in working condition. But he still knew
he was powerless against the mighty armies of Moab and Ammon. So,
he sought out His God. His living faith was proactive, constructive, and
had a mindful mastery of his own weaknesses.

Throughout his reign, he taught his people to rely upon their heavenly God. He reminded them how God had led their forefathers, first in
the wilderness and then in the conquering of Canaan. Now, in this time
of crisis, he turns his people to set their eyes, their hearts, and their
faith to this God who had guided over the years their footsteps, their
decisions, their commitments. The whole nation fasted and prayed that
God would cause their enemies to be confused and self-destructive and
that His mighty name would be glorified.

Today, we must remember how God has intertwined Himself into
our lives and led us to be fruitful servants, so should we remain aware,
alert, and alive to embrace whatever crisis may come upon us. We can
know and be assured God, in His love, will stand by us every moment of
our lives if we would only allow Him access.

In verse 12, Jehoshaphat, whose name means "The Lord judges," is asking his God to judge these enemies and punish them.

My Position

Psalm 71:18, *"Now that I am old and grey, do not abandon me, O God. Let me proclaim your power to this new generation, your mighty miracles to all who come after me."*

I think this verse is speaking to me. I am "old and grey," I have lived many years and yet I have seen the hand of God in my life. I have shared some of those moments where He made His appearance to give me strength to carry on; to give me the mind to be alert and see those passages which He has presented in His Word; to give me the opportunity to share my experience with others so they, too, might gain strength from our heavenly Father.

Unless we are willing to share these stories with others, we will forget them ourselves. We must be ever mindful of the interactions of God in our lives.

God's Position

Psalm 147:4–5, *"He determines the number of the stars; he gives to all of them their names. Great is our Lord, and **abundant in power**; his understanding is beyond measure."* (Emphasis mine.)

Jeremiah 10:12–13, *"But God made the earth **by his power**, and he preserves it by his **wisdom**. With his own **understanding**, he stretched out the heavens. When he speaks in the thunder, the heavens roar with rain. He causes the clouds to rise over the earth. He sends the lightning with the rain and releases the wind from his storehouses."* (Emphasis mine.)

Transliteration: Yahweh is the Maker of the earth by his vigor, the Establisher of the habitance by his wisdom, and by His understanding, He stretched out the heavens.

When He sounds forth His voice, there is a rumble of waters in the heavens, and He brings up vapors from the end of the earth; He makes lightning bolts for the rain and brings forth wind from His treasuries.   Interlinear Scripture Analyzer 3 Beta

Hail is often associated with judgment (Isa. 28:2, 17; 30:30–31; Ezk. 13:11–13; 38:22–23). In the eighth plague, God used not only hail, but fire and lightning as well. God, throughout Exodus, demonstrated His awesome power when He combated the various "deities" of the people and destroyed these gods.

Unfortunately, today, we still have this same problem. We tend to forget we have been created and all around us are attempts at promoting, projecting ourselves into powerful positions, powerful places, powerful status. But we have all been created. The One who is the Creator is the one who has DIVINE POWER—GOD. Until we subject ourselves to His power, we will always run into conflict, struggle, disagreement, battle, argument, discord, tension, controversy, opposition.

Matthew 22:29, *"Your mistake is that you don't know the Scriptures, and you don't know the power of God."*

δυναμιν
ability power

Throughout mankind's history, we have allowed Satan to move against God's Word. We are neglecting the power of God's Word to make changes in our lives; we resist God's power which could make us healthier, more productive, and attain His wisdom (*"the fear of the Lord is the beginning of wisdom"* Prov. 1:7). Compromise, while at times is beneficial, has dominated the decline of principles, purity, productivity, and purpose.

> Romans 1:20, *"For ever since the world was created, people have seen the earth and sky. Through everything God made, they can clearly see his invisible qualities—his eternal power, and divine nature. So, they have no excuse for not knowing God."*

This has been and continues to be the great controversy between Christ and Satan. There is no real power in Satan. Once Satan has used you, abused you, accused you, excused you, confused you, diffused you, bemused you, unfocused you, amused **himself** with you, he refuses to acknowledge your worth and casts you out. He no longer has a use for you. There is no love here.

Jesus, on the other hand, loves us unconditionally, desires only the best for us, and demonstrates this by lifting us up, cleaning us up, cheering us up, holding us up, giving **HIMSELF** up for us, filling our minds up with His goodness, His joy, His graciousness. Giving us a life of abundance. John 10:10 (AMP), *"The thief comes only to steal and kill and destroy. I came that they may have and enjoy life, and have it in abundance [to the full, till it overflows]."*

Who do we give our allegiance to? Who do we want to provide power in our lives today? In the end, this is **our** choice. No one can make this choice for us. We must make this choice on our own. We cannot and must not rely upon our fathers' choice. The choice our fathers made must remain with them. God has no grandchildren, only children. That is God's power in allowing us this choice. Otherwise, Satan would take our choice away from us. Satan has no power so long as we choose to allow God to use HIS mighty power in us.

Questions to Ponder:

Have I experienced the divine power in my own life?

Have I shared this experience with others?

Have I ever turned from God's power and chosen something else? What was the result?

Take Away Notes:

DIVINE PROTECTION

Exodus 12:13, 23, 27: *"The blood will be a sign for you on the houses where you are, and when I see the blood, I will pass over you. No destructive plague will touch you when I strike Egypt.... 'For the Lord will pass through to strike the Egyptians, and when he sees the blood on the lintel and on the two doorposts, the Lord will pass over the door and will not allow the destroyer to enter your houses to strike you...you shall say, "It is the sacrifice of the Lord's Passover, for he passed over the houses of the people of Israel in Egypt, when he struck the Egyptians but spared our houses."' And the people bowed their heads and worshiped."*

For this situation, blood was used as a sign of substitution, which we note in Jesus' death in Hebrews 9:26, 28: *"He has appeared to put away sin by the sacrifice of Himself.... Christ was offered once to bear the sins of many. To those who wait for Him, He will appear the second time, apart from sin, for salvation."*

The divine passing over is not based upon human efforts, but rather, it is God's protection and grace.

Of the first nine plagues, the Israelites did not have to do anything. They had no part in protecting themselves, they were participants in that they experienced the first three plagues; but for the next six plagues, they were observers only. For this final plague, they had a part to play.

They had to take blood and paint it on their door posts and lintels. Why? Painting blood on the doorposts required faith in this divine protection.

Why was it necessary for the doorposts and the lintel be painted with the blood? Could they not just paint the lintel or the doorposts? Why both needed to be painted? Why not just paint the door itself?

Egyptian archeology provides the answer to these questions.

There are five parts to the human being according to Egyptian thinking:

1) The physical body—thus mummification was important. There are many today who fear having parts of their body missing when they die. Thus, they negate God's ability to resurrect them whole.

2) The shadow. They believed that the shadow demonstrated reality and was a very real part of a person's being. The same holds today. Often in movies, we see a ghost who has no shadow, and are led to think and believe the lie that we shall not die.

3) The *"ka"* or "life force." As Christians, we call the force that gives us life "the breath of life" (Gen. 2:7, *"then the Lord God formed the man of dust from the ground and breathed into his nostrils the breath of life, and the man became a living creature"*). Often, this "life force" is considered as a separate entity from the body. It has its own identity. It takes God's breath *combining* with the dust to create a living being, a being who not just lives physically but also mentally, emotionally, and spiritually.

4) The *"ba"* or "character traits." Every created being has a character. This is what makes each one unique. God created each one to have an individual and unique relationship with Him.

5) The name. Without a name, a person is considered a non-entity. Moses, writing about the experience of the Exodus story, demonstrates this rationale. For instance, in Exodus 1:15, he mentions the names of the two midwives who were faithful to God, but ignores Pharaoh's name (Ex. 1:8) because he was rejected by God. Thus, the name is so important.

During the Second World War, the German soldiers, following the orders of their commanders, tattooed numbers upon the prisoners. Whenever roll call took place, they would call out the number, not the name.

Today, we see this phenomenon where people are referred to by their account number, their employee number, their social security number. Rarely do we hear people called by their name.

What Is in a Name?

During a recent visit to a bed and breakfast establishment, I needed to cross the ice road to the island which held the reserve for the indigenous people. As we traveled, I asked my driver his name. He stated, "Oliver, but that is not my real name. Orville is my real name." I was pleasantly surprised and told him that name was also my father's. He went on to explain, while in fourth grade at the residential school he attended, the nun told him his name no longer was Orville but Oliver. I questioned why and he responded he did not really know unless it was to confuse him. On my return to the B&B, I mentioned this to the owner. He also told me he had received not just one name, but several over the course of his stay at the residential school. He explained it was to make sure to drive the Indian out of them.

Today, a name plays an important spot in society. When asking for someone, it is usually the name that is first mentioned. Rarely do we consider a person's occupation, hobbies, recreational pursuits, titles before we seek the name. A person without a name is considered a non-entity. No one enjoys being referred to as a number.

Israelites to Slaves to Israelites

While the Israelites initially lived in tents when they first went to Egypt, after a couple of generations, they began to live in houses. They were not only copying the Egyptian way of living, but also, they were embracing many of their beliefs.

"Egyptologists excavating the Delta region of Egypt (the northern marshland where the Israelites were dwelling) have discovered many of these early New Kingdom doorposts and lintels (dating to the time period of the Exodus)."[39] Not only did there arise a Pharaoh who did not know about Joseph, so there arose amongst the Israelites people who did not know God, people who embraced the religious beliefs of their overseers.

Since the Israelites were now living in houses, they, too, began to adopt many of the beliefs of the Egyptians. Though their houses were probably made of mud brick, they also—following the example and values of the Egyptians—built the door posts and lintel of stone. They, too, wanted to carve their names for posterity purposes, that they would not be forgotten. They probably also began to believe in an afterlife as did the Egyptians.

The more they embraced the ways of the Egyptians, the less they remembered their own past. Soon, they became slaves, slaves without names became of no interest to their taskmasters.

God had several lessons to teach the Israelites, lessons that needed to be unlearned and lessons to be relearned. The plagues were used to teach these lessons: 1) to demonstrate God's superiority over the gods of the Egyptians; 2) to learn to trust God once again; 3) to embrace the stories of their ancestors, namely Abraham, Isaac, and Jacob. Ultimately, one by one, each plague taught them to trust in God, the Creator.

The final plague would teach them a rudimentary lesson about God's plan of salvation. When He asked the Israelites to paint the doorposts and lintels, He was telling them to cover their names with the blood of the Passover lamb. Carving their names into the doorposts would not ensure them of an afterlife, but covering their names with the blood

---

[39]L.S. Baker Jr., "Covered with blood: A better understanding of Exodus 12:7," *Ministry Magazine*, September 2009, accessed February 9, 2020, https://www.ministrymagazine.org/archive/2009/09/covered-with-blood.html.
"For some examples of these, see Labib Habachi, Tell El-Dab'a I: Tell El-Dab'a and Qantir the Site and Its Connection with Avaris and Piramesse (Vienna: Verlag der österreichischen)"

would secure the life of the oldest child of the family. If they did not apply the blood, their oldest child would die.

This is a lesson for us today. Unless our names are written in the Lamb's Book of Life, we have no assurance of an afterlife either. *"And anyone not found written in the Book of Life was cast into the lake of fire"* (Rev. 20:15).

> "It was not enough that the paschal lamb be slain; its blood must be sprinkled upon the doorposts; so, the merits of Christ's blood must be applied to the soul. We must believe, not only that He died for the world, but that He died for us individually. We must appropriate to ourselves the virtue of the atoning sacrifice.... The flesh was to be eaten. It is not enough even that we believe on Christ for the forgiveness of sin; we must by faith be constantly receiving spiritual strength and nourishment from Him through His word. Said Christ, '**Except ye eat the flesh of the Son of man, and drink His blood, ye have no life in you.** *Whoso eateth My flesh, and drinketh My blood, hath eternal life'*"[40] (Jn. 6:53–54, emphasis mine).

Of course, there is more to our walk with God than this, but it all starts here. The Israelites began their Exodus out of Egypt by putting the blood of the Passover lamb over their names, and then continue their walk of faith as they journeyed into the wilderness following God. Throughout their travels, the Israelites were constantly being reminded of God's protection and care.

Testing

Exodus 15:24, *"And the people grumbled against Moses, saying, 'What shall we drink?'"* Within days of leaving Egypt, the people are already complaining. It appears to be in our nature

---

[40] White, *Patriarchs and Prophets*, p. 277

to complain at the first sign of difficulty, disquiet, discomfort, and dread. Again, in chapter 16:2, the people complained, this time, seeking food. *"And the whole congregation of the people of Israel grumbled against Moses and Aaron in the wilderness."*

In society today, we are concerned about hurting, inhibiting, and discipling our children in their mental and character development. Society has a ban on testing and failing/passing our children, especially in the elementary level. Teachers are no longer allowed to discipline or punish a child for poor behavior. There is no allowance for touching a child either.

Recalling my own experience, I had hearing and seeing disabilities. I was a quiet child and placed at the back of the class because I was not a "problem/disciplinary" child. Therefore, because I could not see well or hear well, my grade three and four teachers passed me into the next grade, even though I had not sufficient grades to be passed on to the next grade. Fortunately, the fifth grade teacher recognized the problem and failed me in order to allow me to develop some foundational lessons. Today, I find myself missing out on the occasional foundational requirements.

God tested the people. In Hebrew thinking, to test another is to determine the worthiness of that person and to develop positive qualities in that individual. Another meaning demonstrates something in their personality as well as in God's character.

"They forgot their bitter service in Egypt.

"They forgot the goodness and power of God displayed in their behalf in their deliverance from bondage.

"They forgot how their children had been spared when the destroying angel slew all the first-born of Egypt.

"They forgot the grand exhibition of divine power at the Red Sea.

"They forgot that while they had crossed safely in the path that had been opened for them, the armies of their enemies, attempting to follow them, had been overwhelmed by the waters of the sea."[41] (Emphasis mine.)

Lest we also forget how God has led us in our own past, will we also complain about trivialities, insignificant life experiences, inconsequential elements of everyday living? Ours is to obey God's direction for our lives, place ourselves wholly into His very capable hands, and trust in His wisdom.

Exodus 15:26, *"If you will diligently listen to the voice of the Lord your God, and do that which is right in his eyes, and give ear to his commandments and keep all his statutes, I will put none of the diseases on you that I put on the Egyptians, for I am the Lord, your healer."* God set up guiding principles to begin a new relationship between Himself and Israel. Health plays an important part in this relationship. For further information see Chapter 11, "Divine Healer."

We must go through the same experience as the Israelites. The road may be long, it may be difficult at times, but being covered by the blood of the Lamb ensures us protection and care if we place our trust in the ONE who can protect us. Our obedience demonstrates our allegiance. We cannot do this on our own, in our own power, using our own will, relying upon our own strength.

Our only safety is in constant distrust of self and dependence on Christ.[42]

His Name

Revelation 14:1, *"Then I looked, and behold, on Mount Zion stood the Lamb, and with him 144,000 who had his name and his Father's name written on their foreheads."*

---

[41] White, *Patriarchs and Prophets*, p. 292

[42] White, *Christ's Object Lessons*, p. 155

Some translations omit "his name," but God's name is still written upon the foreheads of the 144,000. What does this name mean? According to Hebrew thinking, name represents character. Therefore, to have the seal or name of God (Rev. 7:1–3) on the forehead means to reflect God's character in life. To place this seal upon the forehead is also an acknowledgement of God's position in one's life. As the mark on the forehead or hand of the wicked denotes thought and action, so the seal would have a similar response. The seal allows for the law of God to be written upon the believer's heart and thus be absorbed into the believer's life.

Questions to Ponder:

Can the body and the breath of God be separated and still function? If the answer is "no," then how can I believe a dead person continues after death?

How many pagan ideas do I embrace?

Whose name am I willing to have "tattooed" "branded" into my forehead?

Take Away Notes:

DIVINE COMMAND

Exodus 12:11–13, 22–28: *"The Lord said to Moses and Aaron in the land of Egypt, 'This month shall be for you the beginning of months. It shall be the first month of the year for you. Tell all the congregation of Israel that on the tenth day of this month every man shall take a lamb according to their fathers' houses, a lamb for a household. And if the household is too small for a lamb, then he and his nearest neighbor shall take according to the number of persons; according to what each can eat you shall make your count for the lamb. Your lamb shall be without blemish, a male a year old. You may take it from the sheep or from the goats, and you shall keep it until the fourteenth day of this month, when the whole assembly of the congregation of Israel shall kill their lambs at twilight.*

'Then they shall take some of the blood and put it on the two doorposts and the lintel of the houses in which they eat it. They shall eat the flesh that night, roasted on the fire; with unleavened bread and bitter herbs they shall eat it. Do not eat any of it raw or boiled in water, but roasted, its head with its legs and its inner parts. And you shall let none of it remain until the morning; anything that remains until the morning you shall burn. In this manner you shall eat it: with your belt fastened, your sandals

on your feet, and your staff in your hand. And you shall eat it in haste. It is the Lord's Passover. For I will pass through the land of Egypt that night, and I will strike all the firstborn in the land of Egypt, both man and beast; and on all the gods of Egypt I will execute judgments: I am the Lord. The blood shall be a sign for you, on the houses where you are. And when I see the blood, I will pass over you, and no plague will befall you to destroy you, when I strike the land of Egypt....'

Then Moses called all the elders of Israel and said to them, 'Go and select lambs for yourselves according to your clans and kill the Passover lamb. Take a bunch of hyssop and dip it in the blood that is in the basin and touch the lintel and the two doorposts with the blood that is in the basin. None of you shall go out of the door of his house until the morning. For the Lord will pass through to strike the Egyptians, and when he sees the blood on the lintel and on the two doorposts, the Lord will pass over the door and will not allow the destroyer to enter your houses to strike you. You shall observe this rite as a statute for you and for your sons forever. And when you come to the land that the Lord will give you, as he has promised, you shall keep this service. And when your children say to you, "What do you mean by this service?" you shall say, "It is the sacrifice of the Lord's Passover, for he passed over the houses of the people of Israel in Egypt, when he struck the Egyptians but spared our houses."' And the people bowed their heads and worshiped. Then the people of Israel went and did so; as the Lord had commanded Moses and Aaron, so they did."

The instructions for the Passover celebration are precise, detailed, specific, intricate, and elaborate. God, following the chain of command, instructed Moses and Aaron, who in turn directed these commands to the Israelites.

1) *"It shall be the first month of the year for you."*

The Passover designates the first day of the Israelite Religious Calendar, which occurs in March/April known as *Nisan*. Today, the Passover celebration has been replaced in the Christian community by Easter to celebrate Christ's death, burial, and resurrection. The civil calendar begins in September/October known as *Tishri*.

2) Passover Lamb: *"On the tenth day of this month every man shall take a lamb..."*

They were to select a blemish free lamb or kid according to the clan size. If the clan was too small, then they were to join with another clan whereby they could then share the lamb/kid. This lamb/kid was to be a male and a year old (verse 5). The New Testament takes up the theme and applies this to Jesus as being the Lamb of God—1 Peter 1:19, *"but with the precious blood of Christ, like that of a lamb without blemish or spot."*

John 1:29 (NIV), *"The next day John saw Jesus coming toward him and said, "Look, the Lamb of God, who takes away the sin of the world!"* Behold, consider, regard, contemplate. John was not telling his listeners to just look," but spend time with God, understanding the importance, the significance, the magnitude of what God was about to do during Jesus' short three and half years of ministry. In the four Gospels, God spells out the import of the Exodus story.

This lamb appears in several roles:

a) The sanctuary lamb of Numbers 28:1–14
b) The conquering lamb of Revelation 5
c) The submissive lamb of Isaiah 53
d) The Passover lamb of Exodus 12

On the tenth day of the first month, the Israelite family was to select a blemish-free lamb and prepare it for the fourteenth day of this first month (*Nisan*). They were to kill the lamb at twilight (sunset), roast the lamb, not boil it nor eat it raw. The lamb was to remain whole, not broken into pieces.

What was left over after they ate that night was to be burned. The Israelites were to eat the roasted lamb fully clothed, with their shoes on their feet and having their staff in their hand. They were to be ready to move forward and outward the moment they heard the signal, the order, the sound of the ram's horn.

Many years later, while under Roman rule, the Israelites took the habit of eating on low couches around a low table. Thus, they took to celebrating the Passover by reclining at the table. It would then have been easy for Jesus to wash the feet of His disciples (Jn. 13:1–17).

3) Hyssop

Hyssop is an herb in the mint family with cleansing, medicinal, and flavoring properties; it was prolific in the Middle East and was used in a variety of ways.

The hyssop used in sprinkling the blood was the symbol of purification, being thus employed in the cleansing of the leper and of those defiled by contact with the dead. In the psalmist's prayer, its significance is also seen: *"Purge me with hyssop, and I shall be clean: wash me, and I shall be whiter than snow"* (Ps. 51:7).[43]

In Leviticus, God commanded His people to use hyssop in the ceremonial cleansing of people and houses. In one example, God tells the priests to use hyssop together with cedar wood, scarlet yarn, and the blood of a clean bird to sprinkle a person recently healed from a skin disease (likely leprosy).

The blood drained from the animal being used for the Passover meal was used to paint the lintel and doorposts. This blood was applied using hyssop.

---

[43] White, *Patriarchs and Prophets*, p. 277

When Jesus was on the cross, He became thirsty due to the loss of His own blood and having had nothing to eat or drink since the night before. John 19:28–30, *"After this, Jesus, knowing that all was now finished, said (to fulfill the Scripture), 'I thirst.' A jar full of sour wine stood there, so they put a sponge full of the sour wine **on a hyssop branch** and held it to his mouth. When Jesus had received the sour wine, he said, 'It is finished,' and he bowed his head and gave up his spirit."* (Emphasis mine.) The use of the hyssop from applying the blood to the doorposts in Egypt, to "purge me with hyssop" (Ps. 51:7), to Jesus seeking a drink of water. Jesus knew that everything had been accomplished and this part of His work was finished; He asked for a drink. The thread of the hyssop completes this segment of Jesus' work.

When He asked the Israelites to paint the doorposts and lintels, He was telling them to cover their names with the blood of the Passover lamb. Carving their names into the doorposts would not ensure them of an afterlife, but in this instance, covering their names with the blood would secure the life of the oldest child of the family. If they did not apply the blood, their oldest child would die.

4) *"In this manner you shall eat it…"*

Your belt fastened – The belt represents truth (Eph. 6:14). Unless we have studied God's Word and gleaned the truth, we cannot be ready to fight the battle soon to come upon us.

Your sandals on your feet – The shoes represent the "gospel of peace" (Eph. 6:15). Preparation for warfare gives us inner peace. Jesus told His disciples in John 14:27, *"Peace I leave with you; my peace I give to you. Not as the world gives do I give to you. Let not your hearts be troubled, neither let them be afraid."* When we have the peace of Jesus within our hearts, we are more than able to join in the battle with Him and can share this peace with those who have never experienced Jesus' peace and friendship.

Your staff in your hand – This represents the sword of the Spirit, which is the Word of God (Eph. 6:17). God provides us with the skills needed to ascertain; to discern the truth in His Word; to understand the beauties, the gems, the grace He wants us to find.

Eat it in haste – *"Oh, taste and see that the LORD is good! Blessed is the man who takes refuge in him!"* (Ps. 34:8). The more we search the Scriptures, the more we find the truth God holds for each of us. The more we find the truth, the more we are drawn to Him. The more we are drawn to God, the more we come to love Him as He first loved us. *"The Lord has appeared of old to me, saying: 'Yes, I have loved you with an everlasting love; Therefore, with lovingkindness I have drawn you'"* (Jer. 31:3 NKJV). Love awakens in the heart of the beholder. Hear His voice and follow Him.

Unleavened bread – This bread was to be eaten along with the roasted lamb. What does unleavened bread represent? "Leavened" usually was associated with sin, so using unleavened bread, this would be considered eating a sinless meal.

5) Do not go outside until morning

"'None of you shall go out of the door of his house until the morning.' [Why?] For the LORD will pass through to strike the Egyptians, and when he sees the blood on the lintel and on the two doorposts, the LORD will pass over the door and will not allow the destroyer to enter your houses to strike you." (Ex. 12:22–23)

God had a job to do, and He did not want nor did He need anyone to interfere. The job of the Israelite was to paint the blood on the doorposts and lintel. Both needed to be covered as we need this today—completely not partially covered. We are to give our **all** to Him before we can be blessed with His forgiveness, His life, His peace. This is the beginning of being "born again."

Judas

In the New Testament, Jesus was celebrating the Passover with His disciples. He had already washed their feet and now He identified His betrayer. John 13:30 states—Judas went out *"and it was night."* Judas left the light of Jesus' teaching, His love, His forgiveness and went out into the darkness.

Nicodemus

John 3 tells of Nicodemus who came to Jesus in the night. Another way we could say this—he came from the darkness into the light of Jesus' presence. Nicodemus had an overwhelming desire to seek the truth, to understand more of what Jesus taught. Paul states in 1 Corinthians 15:1 (KJV), *"I die daily,"* indicating he gave himself every day to the service of His Lord. Otherwise, what is the point of being born again if there is no life after death? In Luke 9:23, Jesus says: *"Then He said to them all, 'If anyone desires to come after Me, let him deny himself, and take up his cross daily, and follow Me.'"*

Two more times Nicodemus shows up in the book of John. The next time we encounter him is in John 7:46–52. The council has gathered in an attempt to stop Jesus and even find a way to put Him to death. Verse 51 quotes him saying: *"Does our law judge a man before it hears him and knows what he is doing?"* Let us not underestimate what is happening here. Nicodemus is testifying on behalf of Jesus. This is the second step of being born again.

The last time we see Nicodemus is in John 19:38–42. Nicodemus is doing a service for His Lord. He, along with Joseph of Arimathea, prepared Jesus' body for burial. He was servicing "the body of Jesus." What does it mean to "service the body of Jesus"? Taking care of the activities within and without the church of Christ.

Nicodemus' story tells us how we can know we are born again.

a) We have an overwhelming desire to connect, to talk with, to be in the presence of Jesus.
b) We testify what Jesus has done, both in and to us to change us from within.
c) We provide service to the "Body of Christ."

6) I WILL

"For I will pass through the land of Egypt that night, and I will strike all the firstborn in the land of Egypt, both man and beast; and on all the gods of Egypt I will execute judgments: I am the LORD." (Ex. 12:12)

Pass through the land – This demonstrates His omnipresence. He is on the move. He is active.

Strike all the firstborn – In Exodus 11:5, God had already told Pharaoh that the firstborn would be slain. This was the final warning to him that God meant business. God's grace had up to this time been great; and in his mercy, God slew the stubborn people without torture.

Execute judgments – These judgments were on the gods of the Egyptians. Throughout the nine plagues God had been demonstrating to the Egyptians as well as the Israelites, the gods of Egypt were impotent, were not alive, had no power within themselves, and thus were not to be feared nor worshiped.

7) The memorial of Passover

Exodus 12:14, *"This day shall be for you a memorial day, and you shall keep it as a feast to the LORD; throughout your generations, as a statute forever, you shall keep it as a feast."*

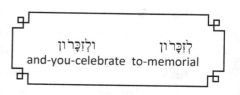

How long is forever? This term is used often by individuals who, in anticipation or anxiety, deem a given activity to occur. The Passover ritual was in effect until the Lamb of God was sacrificed. Jesus fulfilled this Passover ritual at His death on the cross. So, starting at the exodus of Israel from Egypt until the death and resurrection of Jesus, the Passover festival would take place yearly, helping the Israelites to remember how God had guided them, fed them, took care of their clothes, and provided them the health needed to live in the wilderness for those forty years.

In the story of the Last Supper, in the upper room, Jesus instituted a New Covenant service—Communion. What exactly is this Communion? From where did this term come? What has changed, or was there actually a change?

8) Meaning

Unless we understand why we are doing something, it soon becomes a mindless ritual. We no longer need to think about what we are doing or saying, we just do it or say it.

So, it is with the Passover service and today it is the Communion service. Why are we celebrating this service? Unless there is meaning, the service becomes mundane; just go through the process without a second thought, which leads to a casual Christianity.

The Passover consisted of a slain lamb and unleavened bread. The Israelites were to observe this Passover to remember how God freed them from the slavery of Egypt. The lamb was a "guidepost" directing their attention forward to the time when Jesus would appear to die on the cross for them.

The Communion service utilizes the cup of wine and broken unleavened bread. Is there really a difference? Jesus knew His death would replace the slain lamb. He tells us He is the BREAD of LIFE (Jn. 6:35) and the WATER of LIFE (Jn. 4:14). He knew His body would be "broken" for His people—both those who lived before Him and those who would come to know Him down to our time.

The cup of wine replaced the slain lamb. Why? Jesus was the slain Lamb. His blood was spilled on the cross. When He died and the spear was driven into His heart, the blood and water had separated, indicating He died of a broken heart. It was at the Passover meal Jesus changed the format of this service.

As indicated above, the blood painted on the doorposts was an act of faith on the part of the Israelite. Has this been replaced in the service we celebrate today? Yes, it has. We no longer are required to paint our doorposts and lintels with blood to demonstrate our faith. The foot washing service is our service in faith. Accepting the blood of the Lamb (Jesus) covering our sins, we wash each other's feet to demonstrate our service in faith because we have been covered in His blood. This is not just a service of humility, but it is also a service demonstrating our faith in His atoning sacrifice.

The unleavened bread remains—why? Leaven, as described earlier, indicates sin, so we come to this service **after** investigating our own hearts and minds and asking for forgiveness, so we can come to the table with a sinless heart.

9) Go and do likewise

As the Israelites *"went and did so; as the LORD had commanded"* (Ex. 12:28), so today we have been given the command to go and do likewise. As inconvenient it might be to wash each other's feet, we have been commanded to go and do likewise. As unnerving, uncomfortable, scary it might be to tell others about our friend, Jesus, we have been commanded to go and do likewise.

Jesus came to earth to be an example for us; He has given the Holy Spirit to aid us in carrying out the duties He commands of us. He has promised and He still holds to His promise, *"And behold, I am with you always, to the end of the age"* (Matt. 38:20).

While giving the instructions for the Passover, Moses also explained the meaning of this Passover. In the years to come, the children of Israel would hold this feast as a memorial and as a celebration of the providences of God on their behalf. Later, Moses lists this celebration as one of the three main feasts (Lev. 23) they would be expected to participate as part of their worship to God.

Questions to Ponder:

Am I living a casual Christian life?

How can I change from casual to actively participating in sharing the good news to others?

Have I embraced the emblems of the Communion service to my relationship with God?

Take Away Notes:

DIVINE ACTION CAUSES WORSHIP

Exodus 12:27 (NIV), *"tell them, 'It is the Passover sacrifice to the Lord, who passed over the houses of the Israelites in Egypt and spared our homes when he struck down the Egyptians.' Then the people bowed down and worshiped."* God is a God of action. God does not rest and take it easy now that the creation is complete. In John 5:17, Jesus made this statement: *"But Jesus answered them, 'My Father is working until now, and I am working.'"* Jesus was accused of breaking the Sabbath law. He had healed a paralytic man suffering for thirty-six years. Instead of worshiping and praising God for this man's healing, the Jews wanted to kill Him.

The song entitled *I Can Only Imagine* tells of Bart Millard's reaction to his father's change in behavior towards society and himself. From being an abusive man to being considerate, gentle, and kind with any individual he came into contact, his father attributed this change when he came to know Jesus as his Lord and Savior and changed his whole outlook on life. Bart was with his father when death finally claimed him, but during the weeks he spent caring for his father, he began to realize the change in his father was genuine.

Do you recall a time when you recognized God working a miracle in your own life?

What did you do during that experience when you acknowledged God's action?

What did I do?

When I had my accident on highway 101, I took the complete front end my Jeep off. The headlights were hanging crookedly, the grill was gone, the bumper was dangling on one bolt. But I was safe. When I realized I was okay, I laid my head on the steering wheel and thanked God for saving me. I cried, and I looked up from time to time to see that I was okay. For approximately five minutes, I kept thanking God for saving my life as I saw more and more of just what could have happened. Some of the guard posts were broken, there was a steep slope beyond those guard rails; each new piece of information took me back to God, thanking Him for saving me. Realizing the radiator was exposed but not torn brought words of thanks to my lips. My vehicle, as ugly as it was now, was still drivable. God was still acting on my behalf. He was preparing the help I needed.

When transport driver passed me with his rig, I thought he was ignoring me, and my happiness turned to anger to think he would leave me there in the middle of nowhere. When I saw him walking and sliding down the hill toward, me I asked God to forgive me of my instant anger.

Do you remember a time when God intervened in your life? What was your response?

The Bible tells many stories about what the Israelites did when God's action affected their lives.

Exodus 12:27, *"tell them, 'It is the Passover sacrifice to the Lord, who passed over the houses of the Israelites in Egypt and spared our homes when he struck down the Egyptians.' Then the people bowed down and worshiped."*

Before the lamb was selected, before the bread was made, before the packing was commenced, before the doorposts and lintels were painted, the people *"bowed their heads and worshiped."*

Their focus had to be set true, their view had to be corrected, their compass had to be calibrated, their hearts had to be rectified, their minds had to be settled. Settled to knowing God was, still is, will always be in charge. God is a God of action.

If we do not allow God to have charge of our lives, to dwell within our hearts, to work within our minds, our lives will be jumbled, confused, disorientated. Are we willing to take the risk and allow God in?

Exodus 12:28, *"Then the people of Israel went and did so; as the LORD had commanded Moses and Aaron, so they did."*

God's Action Calls Us to Worship

Earlier, the people were compelled to this act of worship when they realized God knew about their plight. Exodus 4:31, *"And when they heard that the Lord was concerned about them and had seen their misery, they bowed down and worshiped."*

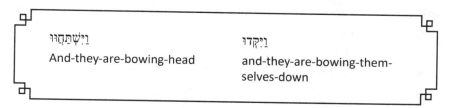

וַיִּשְׁתַּחֲוּוּ
And-they-are-bowing-head

וַיִּקְּדוּ
and-they-are-bowing-them-selves-down

When we realize God has our best interest in hand, we tend to sit back and worship Him, thanking Him for getting us through whatever turmoil we experienced, even during the trial we may be experiencing. The Israelites first encountered this God when Moses told them God knew of their distress; and even while remaining in the midst of their slavery, they still bowed down and worshiped.

After going through the ten plagues, crossing the Red Sea, suffering from thirst, looking for something to eat, they are now camping around the Mount of God—Mount Sinai. The Israelites have gone through so much. So, with the lightning, the thundering, the peeling of the trumpet, when the voice of God speaks from the top of the Mount, they are afraid. They are overwhelmed, they are astonished, they are speechless, they are flabbergasted, they are dumbfounded, so they stand far off and beg Moses to speak to them, not God.

Exodus 20:21, *"The people stood far off, while Moses drew near to the thick darkness where God was."* This was not a reverential, prayer standing far off; this was fear of a mighty God, fear for their lives, fear for their safety, fear for their comfort, fear for their peace of mind. Despite all God had recently done for and with them, they still could not bring themselves to trust this mighty God.

Genesis 3 tells the sad story of Adam and Eve failing to trust God. God would come in the cool of the evening to visit them. On this particular evening, they were nowhere to be found. *"But the Lord God called to the man [אָדָם – adam – human] and said to him, 'Where are you?' And he said, 'I heard the sound of you in the garden, and I was afraid, because I was naked, and I hid myself.'"* Why would God ask this question? Did He not already know where they were? Of course, He did. God asked this question for their benefit. And God asks us today for our benefit. Have I recently checked myself to know where I stand with God?

Fear is part of the sin problem. As Christians today, we have an advantage. Through prayer, we experience God's grace as we learn to trust Him and thus reduce the fear that assails us. We also have hope of the future because of what God completed in the past.

No wonder this song "I Can Only Imagine" is so prevalent, so well-liked, accepted, and admired today. It speaks to each of our hearts. Today, in our blasé lifestyle, we, too, wonder just how much trust can we place in this God. We may not be going through a time of difficulty, and then again, maybe we are going through a trial dealing with unpleasant issues and think God has abandoned us.

The author of this song saw his father's transformation from a corrupt, mean tyrant to a loving, concerned, peaceful man. He struggled to understand what happened. Was this to be short-lived or was this truly a deep change that occurred in his father's life. As time went on, he observed this change was permanent. So, within his own heart, he was trying to imagine his own experience.

What is my response to God's action in my life? What is your response? Only as we continue in our relationship experience with our Father will we be able to begin to comprehend His amazing action in our lives. When He calls us in the wee hours of the morning, rather than complain, we find ourselves worshiping His awesome love as we sense His caring arms around us.

Are there any other examples in the Bible which speak of people worshiping God when He acts?

Eliezer – Servant of Abraham

Genesis 24 tells the story of Abraham's servant when he was sent to Abraham's family to seek a wife for Isaac. We encounter three prayers: The first prayer, the servant stands by the well and asks for God's blessing on his journey (verses 12–13).

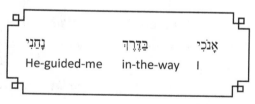

The second prayer, we find in verses 26 and 27—*"Then the man bowed down and worshiped the Lord, saying, 'Praise be to the Lord, the God of my master Abraham, who has not abandoned his kind-*

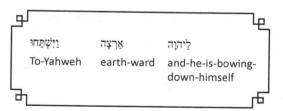

ness and faithfulness to my master. As for me, the Lord has led me on the journey to the house of my master's relatives.'" Eliezer is realizing God is answering his own prayer, not just the prayer of his master, Abraham.

In the third prayer in verse 52, *"When Abraham's servant heard their word, he bowed himself to the earth before the LORD"*

This servant goes from standing, to bowing his head, to

prostrating himself on the ground. As he receives answers to his prayers, step by step, he comes to realize just how much God is willing to bless not just his master, Abraham, but also to bless his own efforts.

Solomon's Temple (2 Chron. 5:13b–14)

The temple has been built and now the Israelites are dedicating this temple to the name of their God. God accepts their sacrifices and consumes them with his own fire and fills the temple with His glory. The priests must move out of the temple because of the cloud of His glory.

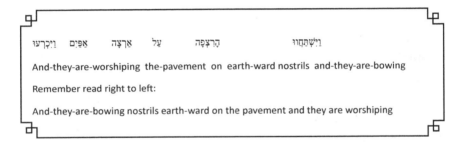

2 Chronicles 7:3, *"When all the Israelites saw the fire coming down and the glory of the Lord above the temple, they knelt on the pavement with their faces to the ground, and they worshiped and gave thanks to the Lord, saying, "He is good; his love endures forever."*

The Israelites not only bowed to the ground, they praised God, declaring His goodness and His love.

Hezekiah Restores Temple Worship

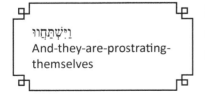

2 Chronicles 29:29, *"When the offerings were finished, the king and everyone present with him knelt down and worshiped."*

Hezekiah had the temple cleansed and repairs completed. Then early in the morning, he, along with the people, went to the temple to worship the LORD, using seven bulls, seven rams, seven lambs, and seven male goats. These offerings covered their sin offerings: kingdom, sanctuary, and Judah.

While the offerings were being burnt on the altar, music was presented as part of the worship. The worship time was not completed yet. The people—individually, in families, and clans—came forward with their offerings and singing. Seventy bulls, one hundred rams, and two hundred lambs were slain a burnt offering; consecration offering had six hundred bulls and three thousand sheep. Included along with these offerings were the peace offerings and drink offerings. *"And Hezekiah and all the people rejoiced, because God had prepared for the people, for the thing came about quickly"* (2 Chron. 29:36).

Absolute worship demands such a response from us. Whenever God does something in our lives, we are compelled, we are constrained, we are induced to respond in kind. Be it bowing our heads, our hearts, our bodies. There can be no indifferent attitude presented.

Ezra Reads the Law

Nehemiah 8:6, *"Ezra praised the Lord, the great God; and all the people lifted their hands and responded, 'Amen! Amen!' Then they bowed down and worshiped the Lord with their faces to the ground."*

First, when Ezra begins to read from the book of the law, the people stood out of respect for the Word of God. Once they had read the law, "Ezra, blessed the LORD," "Ezra, praised the LORD."

The Ultimate Divine Action

All four Gospels record God's action on the cross. Jesus willingly went to the cross for you and me. Despite what appeared to be defeat for Jesus and a win for Satan, the resurrection demonstrated the ultimate win. Eric Liddell once said, "In the dust of defeat as well as the laurels of victory, there is a glory to be found if one has done his best." Suffice it to say, Christ did the ultimate, the very best anyone could and did. His death, burial, and resurrection provide cause for worship on the part of His creation.

Multitude on the Sea of Glass

Revelation 15:2–4 (NIV), *"And I saw what looked like a sea of glass glowing with fire and, standing beside the sea, those who had been victorious over the beast and its image and over the number of its name. They held harps given them by God and sang the song of God's servant Moses and of the Lamb:*

'Great and marvelous are your deeds,
Lord God Almighty.
Just and true are your ways,
King of the nations.
Who will not fear you, Lord,
and bring glory to your name?
For you alone are holy.
All nations will come
and worship before you,
for your righteous acts have been revealed.'"

(Phrases in this song are drawn from Psalm 111:2–3; Deuteronomy 32:4; Jeremiah 10:7; Psalm 86:9 and 98:2.)

To worship before the God of heaven and earth—in the flesh—in person; seeing Him with pure, bright, alert eyes; hearing the multitude singing praises to His mighty Name; lifting our own voices and blending in multiple harmonies with others standing near and far; sharing with each other the stories of God's interventions, God's actions, God's intercessions, God's intermediations, all to save us for that moment, that experience, that occasion, that encounter. "I Can Only Imagine."

Questions to Ponder:

How am I worshiping God today?

Am I demonstrating to God just how thankful I am for His multiple blessings in my own life?

Is my heart in tune and in time with God's actions in my life?

Take Away Notes:

DIVINE OWNERSHIP

Exodus 13:1–2, *"The Lord said to Moses, 'Consecrate [Hallow] to me all the firstborn. Whatever is the first to open the womb among the people of Israel, both of man and of beast, **is mine.'"***
(Emphasis mine.)

The redemption of the firstborn of humans and animals is a key part of the Passover celebrations and a reminder of God's redeeming grace (verses 11–16). Note that this refers only to the firstborn and that it contained a buy-back option (at least in most cases).

The purpose here was to anchor solidly into the minds of the people, the Israelites (and us today), the important concept of Divine ownership. <u>**Israel, as the firstborn**</u> (Ex. 4:22–23, *"Then say to Pharaoh, 'This is what the Lord says: Israel is my firstborn son, and I told you, "Let my son go, so he may worship me." But you refused to let him go; so I will kill your firstborn son.'"*) <u>**belonged to God because of His saving grace**</u>. This has nothing to do with the actual order of birth. Jacob was second born, David was youngest of eight brothers, Judah was fourth born, Levi was third born. We become born of God when we embrace His saving grace, when we acknowledge God as our Father, accept our adoption into the family of God.

Israel was the name given to Jacob after he wrestled with the angel of the Lord. Subsequently, Israel has become the national name for the children of Israel. Jesus is considered firstborn in status, rights, and privileges of all mankind.

Status: Jesus is both Son of God and Son of Man.

Rights: Jesus has always had the right to enter into the presence of His heavenly Father. To determine the ownership of the inhabitants of this world, Jesus declared this right when He died upon the cross of Calvary.

God gave Adam and Eve dominion over this world (Gen. 1:28). When they sinned, they gave away their right to authority over all living beings. Satan took over authority, but Jesus regained that right through His righteous life and death upon the cross.

Privileges: Jesus holds the position of firstborn of all creation. He is granted the honor, the glory, and the power because He created all things and all existence is in His power (Rev. 4:11).

Today, those who belong to God and His family are considered spiritual Israel. We have the status, rights, and privileges granted to the members of God's family, including those of the angels, the seraphim, and other created beings.

In the first chapter, "Divine Holiness," we looked at Exodus 19:10–11, *"the Lord said to Moses, 'Go to the people and consecrate them today and tomorrow and let them wash their garments and be ready for the third day. For on the third day the Lord will come down on Mount Sinai in the sight of all the people.'"*

Preparation for the appearing of the Lord involves outward ritual preparation which reflects inner conviction. Note the importance of sacred space, which later becomes even more significant in the design of the tabernacle/temple. Because of the Lord's presence, a mountain became holy (verses 12–13). Mount Sinai could be considered the first tabernacle for the children of Israel. It was at this mountain where God began the covenant process with His people (chapter 19), where He provided the terms of this covenant (chapter 20), where He confirmed this covenant (chapter 24), where He ratified this covenant with the meal with the elders (chapter 24:9–13), and where He gave the blueprints for the building of the wilderness tabernacle (chapters 25–27).

Thus, was constantly taught the lesson that all defilement must be put away from those who would approach the presence of God.[44]

Who Is God?

When Moses first approached Pharaoh, He stated: *"Thus, says the Lord God of Israel: 'Let my people go, that they may hold a feast to me in the wilderness.' Pharaoh's response? 'Who is the Lord, that I should obey His voice?'"* (Ex. 5:1–2).

The conflict is between the Lord and Pharaoh. When he questioned who God was, we need to understand it was a direct challenge to God. Back in Exodus 3:14, God introduced Himself to Moses. Introducing His name focuses on **being** and **existence**, not on characteristics. Divine presence (not merely existence) may be the most important aspect in this context.

Devils Know God

Mark 1:24, *"What have you to do with us, Jesus of Nazareth? Have you come to destroy us? I know who you are—the Holy One of God."* Jesus was teaching in the synagogue on the Sabbath. A man with an unclean spirit was present. Jesus rebukes the spirit and commands him to *"come out of him"* (Mk. 1:25). While Jesus did not go seeking out these demons, once they acknowledged His presence, He faced them head on (Mk. 5:2, 7:25; Luke 4:33). He demonstrated His authority over them.

---

[44] White, *Patriarchs and Prophets*, p. 350

James 2:18–19, *"But someone will say, 'You have faith and I have works.' Show me your faith apart from your works, and I will show you my faith by my works. You believe that God is one; you do well. Even the demons believe—and shudder!"* "Faith" and "believe" are from the same root. These verses demonstrate the contrast between fear and shuddering and the interactive, personal faith of the believer.

πιστιν belief faith

πιστευουσιν they-are-believing

Post Modern Belief

Today, this question is being asked: "Who is the Lord that I should obey His voice?" All around, people are questioning whether God even exists, never mind giving obedience to Him. The truth about God has become so warped, so misconstrued, His commands so compromised; each one has his/her own opinion of who God is, how God fits into our lives, why God should be considered at all. The lies of Satan are believed because man has ceased to search God's Word and allow God to explain Himself. Because of this illiteracy, because of man's love for himself, because mankind considers himself of more importance over the rest of creation, God is pushed out.

Blessings and Curses

Leviticus 26 and Deuteronomy 28 lists the blessings provided by God to those who commit themselves to Him or curses for those who choose to turn away from Him. Psalm 23:6 tells us, *"Surely goodness and mercy shall follow [us],"* thus, those who seek God and His truth will find the blessings pursuing them. We will not need to seek for these blessings. Matthew 5:33 reveals the motive for these blessings—*"seek first the kingdom of God and all these things* (material treasures, prosperity, emotional peace, quietness of thinking, communion with God Himself, enjoyment of eternal life) *shall be added unto you."*

We make the choice. God granted this power to us right from the beginning, from Creation. Adam and Eve were given the choice of whether they would trust God's command or Satan's lie. They chose Satan's lie. The rest, some might say, is history. But rather than place the blame solely upon Adam and Eve, we must also bear responsibility. We, likewise, have been given the power of choice.

God has never removed this power from any of His creation. Even the angels in heaven have the power of choice. When Lucifer became sin in heaven, he persuaded one third of the angel population to side with him. He and they have taken up their abode here in earth because our forebears elected to listen to him rather than God.

Choosing God

God is the main theme in Exodus, thus it is relational, emotional, and rational (not just intellectual) and it involves commitment.

The Lord worked for His people by signs and wonders, sending terrible judgments upon Pharaoh. At length, the destroying angel was bidden to slay the firstborn of man and beast among the Egyptians. That the Israelites might be spared, they were directed to place upon their doorposts the blood of a slain lamb. Every house was to be marked, so that when the angel came on his mission of death, he might pass over the homes of the Israelites.[45]

In chapter eight, "Divine Command," I have provided detailed information for the Passover. The Israelites had to make the complete commitment to serving God. So today, we also must make this complete commitment to serving God. It is our choice as to who we obey and give allegiance.

Choose this Day

Joshua 24:14–15, *"Now therefore fear the Lord and serve him in sincerity and in*

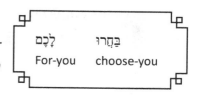

בַּחֲרוּ	לָכֶם
choose-you	For-you

---

[45] White, *The Desire of Ages*, p. 51

113

faithfulness. Put away the gods that your fathers served beyond the River and in Egypt and serve the Lord. And if it is evil in your eyes to serve the Lord, choose this day whom you will serve, whether the gods your fathers served in the region beyond the River, or the gods of the Amorites in whose land you dwell. But as for me and my house, we will serve the Lord."

The choice is ours to make. What an amazing powerful thing God has placed within our hands—choice. Fear God. Serve God. Embrace God. This is the choice God has given to each one of us.

Redeeming the Firstborn

Instead of taking all the firstborn for His service, He selected one tribe to serve Him and His sanctuary.

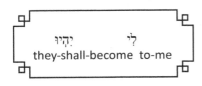

Numbers 3:13, *"Behold, I have taken the Levites from among the people of Israel instead of every firstborn who opens the womb among the people of Israel. The Levites shall be mine, for all the firstborn are mine. On the day that I struck down all the firstborn in the land of Egypt, I consecrated for my own all the firstborn in Israel, both of man and of beast. They shall be mine: I am the Lord."*

"The dedication of the firstborn had its origin in the earliest times. God had promised to give the Firstborn of heaven to save the sinner. This gift was to be acknowledged in every household by the consecration of the firstborn son. He was to be devoted to the priesthood, as a representative of Christ among men."[46]

---

[46] White, *The Desire of Ages*, p. 51

God had saved the firstborn Israelites in Egypt, so He claimed them as His own. Rather than sacrificing these sons, as they were to do to the firstborn of animals, the Israelites were to redeem them by giving something to take their place to the Lord (Ex. 12:29; 13:2, 12–15). Because the firstborn of all the tribes belonged to Him, God could use them as His priests and their assistants.

However, He gave these roles to the Levites because they were loyal to Him at the time of the golden calf apostasy (Ex. 32:25–29; Deut. 10:8).

"Thus, the law for the presentation of the firstborn was made particularly significant. While it was a memorial of the Lord's wonderful deliverance of the children of Israel, it prefigured a greater deliverance, to be wrought out by the only begotten Son of God. As the blood sprinkled on the doorposts had saved the first-born of Israel, so the blood of Christ has power to save the world."[47]

Jesus – The Firstborn

Luke 2:21–24, "And at the end of eight days, when he was circumcised, he was called Jesus, the name given by the angel before he was conceived in the womb. And when the time came for their purification according to the Law of Moses, they brought him up to Jerusalem to present him to the Lord (as it is written in the Law of the Lord, 'Every male who first opens the womb shall be called holy to the Lord') and to offer a sacrifice according to what is said in the Law of the Lord, "a pair of turtledoves, or two young pigeons."

Earlier, John the Baptist (Lk. 1:59) was circumcised and called John, not Zacharias. His father's tongue was loosened when he himself wrote John's name.

---

[47] White, *The Desire of Ages,* p. 51

Jesus' earthly parents were devout Jews and so faithfully adhered to the commands of circumcision and ritual of impurity (Lev. 12:1–8). To present Jesus to the Lord, Joseph and Mary took Jesus to Jerusalem.

"What meaning then was attached to Christ's presentation! But the priest did not see through the veil; he did not read the mystery beyond. The presentation of infants was a common scene. Day after day, the priest received the redemption money as the babes were presented to the Lord. Day after day, he went through the routine of his work, giving little heed to the parents or children, unless he saw some indication of the wealth or high rank of the parents. Joseph and Mary were poor; and when they came with their child, the priests saw only a man and woman dressed as Galileans, and in the humblest garments. There was nothing in their appearance to attract attention, and they presented only the offering made by the poorer classes."[48]

The priests were blinded by ritual and did not seek to discover God's truth. They were only interested in temporal wealth, earthly status, worldly recognition. They did not have their eyes fixed upon God, they did not seek spiritual guidance, they did not grasp eternal values and truths as important.

Today, we must consider every ritual, every service, every ceremony has meaning; otherwise, we perform these sacraments, these ordinances with disdain, disinterest, and disregard.

Following the deliverance of the firstborn of Israel in Egypt, during the tenth and final plague, God directed Moses that all firstborn of human and animal belonged to Him. It would take the blood of the lamb to redeem the human firstborn. (Passover—Exodus 12:3–13; consecration of firstborn—Exodus 13:11–15; and separation of Levites for service in the sanctuary—Numbers 8:13–18.)

---

[48]White, *The Desire of Ages,* p. 52

Jesus came to earth not just to redeem the Israelites, but all mankind. According to Colossians1:15–17, *"He is the image of the invisible God, the firstborn of all creation. For by him all things were created, in heaven and on earth, visible and invisible, whether thrones or dominions or rulers or authorities—all things were created through him and for him. And he is before all things, and in him all things hold together."*

Herein are two central aspects—creation and redemption. Colossae, at that time, was stressing the importance of other powers, thus diminishing the significance of Jesus. Paul needed to correct this assertion. Jesus, being the firstborn, not in literal birth order, though He was through Mary, but about the privileges and rights of the firstborn son.

When we devalue Jesus' position, we are making a choice. When we cheapen salvation's plan, we are making a choice. When we belittle those who decide to follow Jesus and make His precepts their own, we are making a choice.

"We are fallen human beings, and if left to our own devices, if left to follow the inclinations of our hearts, we'll surely wander from the path that God calls us to walk on."[49]

Questions to Ponder:

Am I willing to place my trust in God's hands?

How do I demonstrate my loyalty, my faith, my belief in and to God?

What choices have I made in the past that are detrimental to my life today?

Am I willing to place these poor choices into God's hands today for Him to handle my life?

Take Away Notes:

_____

[49] *Adult Sabbath School Bible Study Guide,* Fourth Quarter, (2018), p. 16

DIVINE HEALER

Exodus 15:25b–26, *"There the Lord made for them a statute and a rule, and there he tested them, saying, 'If you will diligently listen to the voice of the Lord your God, and do that which is right in His eyes, and give ear to His commandments and keep all His statutes, I will put none of the diseases on you that I put on the Egyptians, for I am the Lord, your healer.'"*

God introduces Himself to the people, telling them He is Jehovah-Rapha— He can heal physically, mentally, and spiritually. He heals completely, making us whole again. *"God shows* [demonstrates]

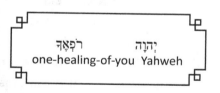

רֹפְאֶךָ   יְהוָה
one-healing-of-you   Yahweh

his love for us in that while we were still sinners, [while we were still broken, while we were still incomplete, while we were separated from HIM] *Christ died for us"* (Rom. 5:8). *"All this is from God, who through Christ reconciled us to himself and gave us the ministry of reconciliation"* (2 Cor. 5:18).

"Grace is an attribute of God exercised toward undeserving human beings. We did not seek for it, but it was sent in search of us. God rejoices to bestow His grace upon us, not because we are worthy, but because we are so utterly unworthy. Our only claim to His mercy is our great need."[50]

The children of Israel had recently left Egypt. We have not been told how long it took them to reach the Red Sea. Suffice it to say, transporting 1.5 million people carrying all their belongings, plus the plunder of Egypt, it would take time. Also, we must consider the Egyptians themselves have been decimated of their wealth and are in the depths of sorrow from losing their firstborn children. This includes Pharaoh as well.

They had food and water when they left, but now, three days *after* crossing the Red Sea, they are getting very low on water. They arrive at Marah, but the water is bitter. The people complain. They are confused. They are puzzled. They are perplexed as to why God would bring them to a place where the water was not drinkable. Three days earlier, they were singing praises to the God of their fathers. Now, they were complaining about lack of potable water.

God told them if they would listen to Him, follow His paths, they would grow in a relationship with Him. God wanted them for His own special people. He was willing to help them trust Him; He was willing to heal them spiritually. But they have been given the power of choice.

God desires to have a relationship with us today. He longs to see us complete—physically, mentally, socially, and spiritually. He yearns a restoration of what was in the beginning; trust, confidence in His ability to care for us; to watch us grow in grace, faith, and love.

God tells Moses to put a log into the water and the water is now drinkable. No more impurities, no more contamination, nor any pollution. God has healed the waters. As God healed the water, God also wanted to heal their minds, reassuring them He was with them, encouraging them to listen to Him and follow Him.

God is establishing the foundational values for having a relationship between Himself and His people, both in Israel's time as well as today.

---

[50]White, *The Ministry of Healing*, p. 161

Health is important to God and thus it should be important to us as well. But health is more than just physical, it also includes mental, emotional, social, and spiritual health.

> "[Jesus] taught that disease is the result of violating God's laws, both natural and spiritual. The great misery in the world would not exist did men but live in harmony with the Creator's plan."[51]

In the chapter on "Divine Consent" and "Divine Denial," we will encounter the idea of the people doing things "in their own eyes."

> Proverbs 14:12, *"There is a way that seems right to a man, but its end is the way of death."*

> "It is the first and highest duty of every rational being to learn from the scriptures what is truth, and then to walk in the light and encourage others to follow his example. We should day by day study the Bible diligently, weighing every thought and comparing scripture with scripture. **With divine help we are to form our opinions for ourselves as we are to answer for ourselves before God."**[52] (Emphasis mine.)

A) What Is Right in HIS Eyes

Christ had been the guide and teacher of ancient Israel, and He taught them that health is the reward of obedience to the laws of God. The Great Physician who healed the sick in Palestine had spoken to His people from the pillar of cloud, telling them what they must do, and what God would do for them.[53]

---

[51] White, *The Desire of Ages,* p. 824

[52] Ellen G. White, *The Great Controversy between Christ and Satan,* (Oshawa, ON: Pacific Press Publishing Association, 1950), p. 598.

[53] White, *The Desire of Ages,* p. 824

Proverbs 3:7, *"Be not wise in your own eyes, fear the Lord, and turn from evil."*

Christ, in His life, made no plans for Himself. He accepted God's plans for Him, and day by day, the Father unfolded His plans. So should we depend upon God that our lives may be the outworking of His will? As we commit our ways to Him, He will direct our steps.[54]

Living well and doing right require perseverance and spiritual direction. Where do we find this spiritual direction? The obvious answer would be the scriptures.

Colossians 3:1–4, *"If then you have been raised with Christ, seek the things that are above, where Christ is, seated at the right hand of God. Set your minds on things that are above, not on things that are on earth. For you have died, and your life is hidden with Christ in God. When Christ who is your [our] life appears, then you [we] also will appear with him in glory."*

i) Raised with Christ

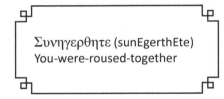

Συνηγερθητε (sunEgerthEte)
You-were-roused-together

"Singleness of purpose, wholehearted devotion to God, is the condition pointed out by the Savior's words…. Real piety begins when all compromise with sin is at an end."[55]

If this means we must give up a bad habit, so be it. We are to constantly strive, continuously struggle, persistently fight the good fight, forever be on alert for those things which will trip us up and cause us to fall. We must be mindful of the teachings of Jesus, attentive to His

---

[54]White, *The Ministry of Healing,* p. 479

[55]Ellen G. White, *The Mount of Blessings,* (Oshawa, ON: Pacific Press Publishing Association, 1955), p. 91.

leading, heedful to follow in His footsteps, not running ahead of both Him and our thoughts.

ii) Seek the Things That Are Above

He who desires to know the truth must be willing to accept all that it reveals. He can make no compromise with error. To be wavering and halfhearted in allegiance to truth is to choose the darkness of error and satanic delusion.[56]

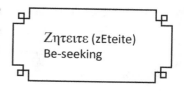

Ζητειτε (zEteite)
Be-seeking

As God fills our minds with His truth, He still gives us the choice of accepting or rejecting that truth. While the truth may be uncomfortable, while the reality of God's grace and mercy may at times seem painful, we must decide whether we want to embrace His truth and draw near to His love, His support, His strength to make those changes in our lives.

iii) Set Your Minds on Things That Are Above

"The follower of Christ will meet with spiritualistic interpretations of the Scriptures, but he is not to accept them. He is to discard all ideas that are not in harmony with Christ's teaching. He is to regard the Bible as the voice of God speaking directly to him."[57]

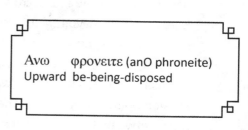

Ανω   φρονειτε (anO phroneite)
Upward be-being-disposed

Even when good Christians present their own understanding of Scripture based upon their own research, each one of us must study

---

[56] White, *The Ministry of Healing,* p. 150

[57] Ellen G. White, *From Trials to Triumph,* (Oshawa, ON: Pacific Press Publishing Association, 1984), P. 250.

for ourselves these truths. After our own research, it then becomes our own and we present this to God Himself. If we have erred, God Himself will correct our thinking, provided we have placed our "minds on things that are above."

I have been researching these past several months the book of Exodus. I am sharing with you through my writing the thoughts of my research. With God's guidance, communicating with Him through prayer and walking with Him, listening to His voice, I am also praying the words I am presenting are truth—God's truth.

iv) Your Life Hidden with Christ

Ζωη υμων κεκρυπται
(zoE humon kekruptai)
Life of-you has-been-hid

A well-known—and told many times—story of a life hidden in Christ:

"After forty years of faithful service overseas, Henry Morrison and his wife were returning to NY due to age and failing health. As the ship they were on approached the dock in NY, they saw a huge crowd waiting and cheering and for a moment Henry thought maybe their labor hadn't gone unnoticed, but they soon realized that the crowd was there for President Theodore Roosevelt who was on the same ship returning from a big game hunting trip to Africa.

As the missionary couple walked to the one room apartment their mission board had provided them, Henry was struggling with the contrast between their unnoticed return after decades of serving God faithfully and the fanfare President Roosevelt received for a couple weeks of hunting. 'It doesn't seem right' he said to his wife. Weeks later he was still so troubled by the thought that they had given their lives in service to the Lord and no one seemed to care or notice that his wife said to him, 'Henry, God doesn't mind if we honestly question Him, but you need to tell the Lord what's on your heart and get this settled.'

So, Henry went to his room and got on his knees and poured out his heart to the Lord. After a while he came out and his wife could see by the peace on Henry's face that the issue had been settled in his heart. 'What happened?' she asked. 'I told the Lord how bitter I was that the president received this tremendous homecoming, but no one even met us at the dock when we returned home. Then the Lord spoke to my heart and said, *Henry, you're not home yet!*'"[58]

While we are here on earth, we will never be able to say we are finally home. There is always a spot in our hearts which tells us we do not belong here. So, we must recognize God has placed us where we are currently and accept His leading, His guiding, His directing in our lives.

Colossians 3: 23–24, *"Whatever you do, work heartily, as for the Lord and not for men, knowing that from the Lord you will receive the inheritance as your reward. You are serving the Lord Christ."*

If we have placed our whole heart, whole soul, whole mind, and whole strength upon God, we will trust Him to bring us through each experience, both positive and negative. We must remember He is WITH us. He does not open a door and shove us through. He opens the door, takes our hand, and walks through that door, facing together that encounter, that event with us. He will not leave us to handle anything completely on our own.

Only as we turn our backs upon Him will we find ourselves dealing with the issue on our own. But He is there the moment we cry out to Him, seeking His help (Matt. 14:22–33). Peter "had always thought of faith as vague and indefinable, and yet it was holding him up now, physically supporting his entire weight as he strolled on the surface of the sea."[59] It was when he turned away from Jesus, He began to sink. It was when he wanted to see what others were observing of his feat, he splashed into the sea. Yet Jesus was nearby, ready and willing to help him, only if he asked.

---

[58] Allen Snapp, "Setting Our Minds on Things Above," Grace Community Church, July 30, 2017, accessed February 9, 2020, https://www.gracecorning.org/sermons/sermon/2017-07-30/setting-our-minds-on-things-above.

[59] Noni Beth Gibbs, *Peter: Fisher of Men*, (Oshawa, ON: Pacific Press Publishing Association, 2007), p. 243.

Matthew 6:22–23, *"The eye is the lamp of the body. So, if your eye is healthy, your whole body will be full of light, but if your eye is bad, your whole body will be full of darkness. If then the light in you is darkness, how great is the darkness!"*

Beholding Jesus we change our viewpoint, our perspective, our understanding. We embrace the beauty of the Savior as we draw nearer to the light He willingly provides. We see His glory as we open ourselves to His teaching, His love, and His leading. We thrill with the wonders He gives so generously. We run out of words to utter our praise and bow before this King of kings in adoration.

B) Give Ear to His Commandments

תִּשְׁמַע   שָׁמוֹעַ
You-are-listening   to-listen
(Diligently listen)

Listen to His Words, His Commandments. First God says, *"diligently listen to the voice of the Lord your God,"* then He says, *"give ear to His commandments."* According to Hebrew scholars, an emphasis is being presented when the same word is repeated.

Jesus, in telling His stories, would often state, *"He who has ears to hear"* (Matt. 11:15; Mk. 4:9).

For most of the world's population, all have in this common—ears. But what we do with these ears is what makes us different from each other. Some pierce, a few will cut, certain ones are lacking the hearing ability, some listen intently, various others doze while listening, and many do additional things while listening. Consequently, the message of the WORD penetrates some ears, while the WORD skims over the surface of the ear, and others absorbs only smidgens of the WORD.

We have been admonished to diligently give, to pay attention, to absorb the truth as presented. God has so much He wants and desires to share with us, His creation. His second book, nature, struggles to listen to their Creator, while we, who were to have dominion over nature has fallen woefully. Nature demonstrates God's love, God's grace, God's mercy, God's forgiveness, God's glory. God greatly desires to share His glory with us. We must diligently listen to His voice, we must seek His truth, we must obey His WORD—not partially, not incompletely, not moderately, but wholeheartedly, fully committed, and enthusiastically

In Revelation (2:7, 11, 15; 3:6, 13, 22), this phrase takes on a life of its own. With each rendering of this expression, the reader should be impressed to pay very close attention and seek God's wisdom concerning what's written. We are expected to understand and then embrace the teaching of the Revelation of Jesus Himself.

C) Keep ALL His Statutes

Deuteronomy 6:1–9, "'Now this is the commandment—the statutes and the rules—that the Lord your God commanded me to teach you, that you may do them in the land to which you are going over, to possess it, that you may fear the Lord your God, you and your son and your son's son, by keeping all his statutes and his commandments, which I command you, all the days of your life, and that your days may be long. Hear therefore, O Israel, and be careful to do them, that it may go well with you, and that you may multiply greatly, as the Lord, the God of your fathers, has promised you, in a land flowing with milk and honey. 'Hear, O Israel: The Lord our God, the Lord is one. You shall love the Lord your God with all your heart and with all your soul and with all your might. And these words that I command you today shall be on your heart. You shall teach them diligently to your children and shall talk of them when you sit in your house, and when you walk by the way, and when you lie down, and when you rise. You shall bind them as a sign on your hand, and they shall be as frontlets between your eyes. You shall write them on the doorposts of your house and on your gates.'"

We touch on this passage in the chapter "Divine Origin." This proclamation became the center of Jewish worship and acknowledges the unity of God. It recognizes the First Commandment—

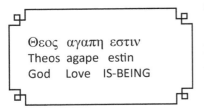

Θεος αγαπη εστιν
Theos agape estin
God Love IS-BEING

"You shall have no other gods before me" (Ex. 20:3). Only God is to be worshiped, only God is to be loved. We demonstrate our love for God by giving to Him the love He already gave to us. First John 4:7–8, *"Beloved, let us love one another, for love is from God, and whoever loves has been born of God and knows God. Anyone who does not love does not know God, because God is love."*

When we consider the commandments of God, we must first and foremost give emphasis to the character of God—LOVE. This LOVE is more than a fundamental character of God; His BEING is LOVE. As fallen creatures of God, we cannot hope to understand this concept, much less observe and keep His commandments, His statutes, His precepts while using our own efforts. It is this LOVE we must somehow embrace, take hold; allow it to fill our own being until His love becomes our love.

God's Statutes:

1. Love God (with your heart, soul, and might)—by loving God in such a way, everything else will follow.
2. Listen to God's voice and His commandments.
3. Seek God entirely; focus on His commandments.
4. Do what God considers to be right; walk in God's ways.
5. Obey God's laws, testimonies, and righteous rules.
6. Commit no wrong.[60]

---

[60]Allison Boutwell, "What Are God's Statutes?" Can I Make It?, February 19, 2015, accessed February 9, 2020, https://allisonlboutwell.wordpress.com/2015/02/19/what-are-gods-statutes/.

I AM the LORD, Your Healer

Deuteronomy 7:15, *"And the Lord will take away from you all sickness, and none of the evil diseases of Egypt, which you knew, will he inflict on you, but he will lay them on all who hate you."*

The sixth plague brought boils upon the Egyptians. When God had Moses toss the soot into the air, He was demonstrating to the Egyptians their gods' inability to prevent disease.

Exodus 23:25, *"You shall serve the Lord your God, and he will bless your bread and your water, and I will take sickness away from among you."* God has promised surety for those who seek Him, who follow His statutes and precepts. His peace, His comfort, His presence are ours as we enter into this covenant relationship with our mighty God.

Second Chronicles 7:14, *"if my people who are called by my name humble themselves and pray and seek my face and turn from their wicked ways, then I will hear from heaven and will forgive their sin and heal their land."* God is willing to be found by His people who seek for Him. He is eager to maintain a relationship with each of His creation.

Questions to Ponder:

Am I seeking God?

Am I willing to listen to His voice, His Word?

Am I eager to follow in His footsteps, do what is right in HIS eyes?

Do I seek to be healed not just physically, but mentally and spiritually?

Take Away Notes:

DIVINE RELATIONSHIP

Exodus 19:5–6, *"Now therefore, if you will indeed obey my voice and keep my covenant, you shall be my treasured possession among all peoples, for all the earth is mine; and you shall be to me a kingdom of priests and a holy nation."*

It takes two to make a relationship. While it might appear a relationship with oneself is possible, it usually does take at least two beings to develop a connection, a bond. God created man for relationship. Not because He was One, but three in One. God is love, therefore He created for companionship, not only for Himself, but also for each created being. This includes the angels, the seraphim, the elders, all creation.

As God taught our first parents the art of relationship, He must have enjoyed their reactions as they came to understand their own concepts of what relationship entails. Relationship is NOT a "one-way street." As Isaiah tells us in chapter 1:18, *"Come now, let us reason together."* Share thoughts, engage in conversation, explore new ideas together, these all rely upon a communion of opinions, considerations, conjectures from each other. It is a sharing between each other of time, space, and actions.

Is there always agreement? No.

Is there always understanding? No.

"Let's agree to disagree." Where did this concept, this phrase come from? The story is told of the friendship between George Whitefield and John Wesley, who both attended Oxford University in England. While they became close friends, they are known to be the originators of the Methodist Church today. They each had their own ideas of God, His world, His plans for their lives. They had many discussions, until finally, one day, one said to the other, "Let's agree to disagree." They would not allow their differences to destroy their friendship, the relationship they had established with each other.

Consequently, it will take many more interactions to be experienced for complete agreement and absolute understanding. It will take all eternity to reach this moment.

God surrounds Himself with His creation. Exodus 25:8, *"And let them make me a sanctuary, that I may dwell in their midst."*

Revelation 4:6–11, *"Around the throne, on each side of the throne, are four living creatures, full of eyes in front and behind: the first living creature like a lion, the second living creature like an ox, the third living creature with the face of a man, and the fourth living creature like an eagle in flight. And the four living creatures, each of them with six wings, are full of eyes all around and within, and day and night they never cease to say,*

Αγιος hagios Holy
קָדוֹשׁ qdush holy-one (Is. 6:3)

'Holy, holy, holy, is the Lord God Almighty, who was and is and is to come!'

["Holy, holy, holy is the Lord of hosts; the whole earth is full of His glory 9Isa. 6:3).]

And whenever the living creatures give glory and honor and thanks to him who is seated on the throne, who lives forever and ever, the twenty-four elders fall down before him who is seated on the throne and worship him who lives forever and ever. They cast their crowns before the throne, saying,

> *'Worthy are you, our Lord and God,*
> *to receive glory and honor and power,*
> *for you created all things,*
> *and by your will they existed and were created.'"*

The created are eager to worship the Creator, they have come before His presence to breathe in His essence, His love, His omnipresence, His omnipotence, His holiness. They willingly surrender their authority to the ONE who deserves and is worthy of worship. He is after all the Creator!

Israel's Relationship with God

Exodus 19:5–6, *"Now therefore, if you will indeed obey my voice and keep my covenant, you shall be my treasured possession among all peoples, for all the earth is mine; and you shall be to me a kingdom of priests and a holy nation."*

Up to this time and place at Mount Sinai, the children of Israel have been observing the plagues poured out upon the Egyptians; they have participated in the first service of Passover; they have crossed over the Red Sea on dry land; they have complained about the lack of water and experienced the gift of that water. They grumbled about the lack of food and encountered manna. The collection of the manna would help them to relearn the importance of the Sabbath. As slaves, they were not given the day to worship.

Before God presented the Ten Commandments, He now comes before them and instructs them to obey His commands and He, God, will make them into a "treasured possession."

"It was God's purpose that by the revelation of His character through Israel, men should be drawn unto Him. To all the world, the gospel invitation was to be given. Through the teaching of the sacrificial service, Christ was to be uplifted before the nations, and all who would look unto Him should live."[61]

Jesus Himself tells us in John 12:32, *"And I, when I am lifted up from the earth, will draw all people to myself."*

"The drawing unto Himself is the assertion of His reign over the world, from which the prince of evil shall be cast out. He will Himself be the centre of the new kingdom, from which none shall be shut out."[62]

"God does not enjoy destroying His creation, He has no delight in the sacrifices and rituals of His people (Ezk. 33:11). The Lord seeks to save, not destroy. He delights in the rescue of sinners.... By warnings and entreaties, He calls the wayward to cease from their evil-doing and to turn to Him and live."[63] He craves companionship, so He took the children of Israel out of Egypt, out of bondage, to teach them His requirements, to share His love for them and subsequently, His whole creation. He wanted to give the children of Israel the opportunity to enter into fellowship with Himself.

First Peter 2:9, *"But you are a chosen race, a royal priesthood, a holy nation, a people for his own possession, that you may proclaim the excellencies of him who called you out of darkness into his marvelous light."*

---

[61] White, *Prophets and Kings,* p. 19

[62] "John 12:32, Ellicott's Commentary for English Readers," Biblehub, accessed February 9, 2020, https://biblehub.com/commentaries/john/12-32.htm.

[63] White, *Prophets and Kings,* p. 105

Because of their failure to carry out God's mandate, He shifted the opportunity to the Gentiles of Jesus' day and into our day to experience this companionship He so desires. The church is God's appointed agency for the salvation of mankind.[64]

Adam and Eve

Adam and Eve tried to hide themselves with fig leaves, demonstrating the broken relationship between themselves and diminishing the image of God in which they had been created. After eating the fruit, *"their eyes were opened, and they suddenly felt shame at their nakedness"* (Gen. 3:7 NLT). They tried to cobble something together flimsy garments to cover their shame, afraid they would be exposed.[65]

When God formed man, God worked in tangent with each other. Together they created man in His image. When He breathed into this first man, Adam, He breathed not just oxygen so the lungs would begin to function, but He instilled His Spirit into him:

SPIRIT OF TRUTH – John 14:16–17, *"And I will ask the Father, and he will give you another Helper, to be with you forever, even the Spirit of truth, whom the world cannot receive, because it neither sees him nor knows him. You know him, for he dwells with you and will be in you."*

When we commune with God, it should be our desire to know HIS truth, not ours as we think it should be. Many have suggested the Bible is God's Word, and they are correct. Saying this, His Word is also understandable by any who desire to seek to understand. When we open the Bible our first thought is to be to the ONE who wrote it, asking Him to open our minds to His teaching. Sometimes we may struggle to

---

[64] White, *The Acts of the Apostles,* p. 127

[65] Nathan Brown, *For the Least of These,* (Nampa, ID: Pacific Press, 2018), p. 21.

understand, but it comes through seeking, asking and knocking at God's heart for His truth (Matt. 7:7–8).

> SPIRIT OF CONVICTION – John 16:8, *"And when he comes, he will convict the world concerning sin and righteousness and judgment"*; Philippians 1:9–10, *"And it is my prayer that your love may abound more and more, with knowledge and all discernment, so that you may approve what is excellent, and so be pure and blameless for the day of Christ."*

It is through the Holy Spirit we are convicted to not only to confess our sins, but also to accept the Truth God is wanting us to learn. Sometimes we wrestle with the Holy Spirit as He teaches us these new truths. God has promised not only to forgive our sins, but through His cleansing power, He makes us holy as He is.

> SPIRIT OF REASON – Isaiah 1:18, *"Come now, let us reason together, says the Lord: your sins are like scarlet, they shall be as white as snow; though they are red like crimson, they shall become like wool."* Romans 12:2, *"Do not be conformed to this world, but be transformed by the renewal of your mind, that by testing you may discern what is the will of God, what is good and acceptable and perfect."*

As we pursue, as we seek, as we search, as we encounter God and His awesome love and truth, we accept His companionship in our lives. The more we learn, the closer we come to know this mighty God, our Creator, our Redeemer; and the closer we come to know Him, the more we find our love blooming for Him. We need to commune daily, to share day to day our thoughts, our concerns, our love, and adoration for this God who created us and then "threw away the mold." His love for each one is unique, one of a kind experience.

SPIRIT OF GRACE – Second Corinthians 12:9, *"But he said to me, 'My grace is sufficient for you, for my power is made perfect in weakness.' Therefore, I will boast all the more gladly of my weaknesses, so that the power of Christ may rest upon me."*

As He showers us with His grace, we also shower others with that same grace, thus we find ourselves in communion throughout our lives not only with God alone, but with our fellow humans. Breaking down the walls of our theories, our prejudices, our religions brings unity and companionship not only with God, but also with each other.

SPIRIT OF FORGIVENESS – Matthew 18:21–22, *"Then Peter came up and said to him, 'Lord, how often will my brother sin against me, and I forgive him? As many as seven times?' Jesus said to him, 'I do not say to you seven times, but seventy-seven times.'"*

Peter, in asking this question thought he would be approved by Jesus when he utilized seven times for forgiveness. The Jewish nation considered three times forgiveness for the same sin to be adequate. Jesus considered unlimited forgiveness.

While we seek to correct the errors of a brother, the Spirit of Christ will lead us to shield him as far as possible from the criticism of even his own brethren—how much more from the censure of the unbelieving world? We ourselves are erring and need Christ's pity and forgiveness, and just as we wish Him to deal with us, He bids us deal with one another.[66]

SPIRIT OF DISCERNMENT – First Corinthians 2:14, *"The natural person does not accept the things of the Spirit of God, for they are folly to him, and he is not able to understand them because*

---

[66] White, *The Desire of Ages*, p. 441

they are spiritually discerned." Proverbs 18:15, *"An intelligent heart acquires knowledge, and the ear of the wise seeks knowledge."*

It must be remembered the discernment of the spirit requires the Holy Spirit's guidance, and therefore, we must request the Holy Spirit's counsel as we search out the Scripture for God's truth. When we place our traditions, our maxims, our requirements above God's conditions, we are placing ourselves in a precarious position. The treasures of God's Word will be hidden from us.

> SPIRIT OF WISDOM – James 1:5, *"If any of you lacks wisdom, let him ask God, who gives generously to all without reproach, and it will be given him."* Proverbs 2:1–5, *"My son, if you receive my words and treasure up my commandments with you, making your ear attentive to wisdom and inclining your heart to understanding; yes, if you call out for insight and raise your voice for understanding, 4 if you seek it like silver and search for it as for hidden treasures, then you will understand the fear of the Lord and find the knowledge of God."*

All these and more were breathed into Adam and Eve. When they sinned, the spirit within them was the first to suffer decay and death. They lost their covering of light (Gen. 3:7). Consequently, David summed it well when he prayed in Psalm 51:10—*"Create in me a clean heart, O God, and renew a right [steadfast] spirit within me."* (Reestablish a relationship within me.)

> "We need to have far less confidence in what man can do and far more confidence in what God can do for every believing soul. He longs to have you reach after Him by faith. He longs to have you expect great things from Him. He longs to give you understanding in temporal as well as in spiritual matters. He can

sharpen the intellect. He can give tact and skill. Put your talents into the work, ask God for wisdom, and it will be given you."[67]

Proverbs 3:1–6, *"My son, do not forget my teaching, but keep my commands in your heart, for they will prolong your life many years and bring you peace and prosperity. Let love and faithfulness never leave you; bind them around your neck, write them on the tablet of your heart. Then you will win favor and a good name in the sight of God and man.* **Trust in the Lord with all your heart and lean not on your own understanding; in all your ways submit to him, and he will make your paths straight."** (Emphasis mine.)

When the children of Israel dwelled in Egypt, they began to integrate into the society surrounding them. They embraced the religious, the societal, the physical attributes of the people of Egypt. Eventually, when they were enslaved by the Egyptians, they did not have the strength to resist because they had compromised their beliefs in their Creator God.

My Treasured Possession

God considered His people as valuable. That is why He went to such great lengths to free them from slavery. That is why He allowed His Son to come to this earth to die upon the cross to make atonement for each one of us.

God validated His love to us and confirmed our worth to Himself by offering the highest payment He could possibly pay. The God who made all the precious jewels, the gold, and the silver has selected us to be His most *treasured possession*. We may not consider ourselves as valuable, we may not consider our deeds as having substance, but God was willing to pay an astronomical price for us to come home.

---

[67] White, *Christ's Object Lessons,* p. 146

To continue looking down upon our self, to continue to abase our-selves through ritual self-destruction only distorts the Creator Himself.

A Kingdom of Priests and a Holy Nation

He desires for us to be a kingdom of priests and a Holy Nation. God has great plans for His people. While Satan appears at times to have the upper hand, the greater victory, we must not forget that with God, He has the final word.

God designed Israel to be a theocracy, a nation governed by Himself through His priests, prophets, and divinely appointed governors. Thus, Israel as a nation chosen by God was responsible for carrying out the duties of educating, blessing, performing sacrifices, and exercising judg-ment of Torah.

Duties/Responsibilities

Malachi 2:7, *"For the lips of a priest should guard knowledge, and people should seek instruction from his mouth, for he is the messenger of the Lord of hosts."* A faithful priest lives as he/she teaches. But with-out love, word and work will be in vain. Walking on the shore of Galilee, Jesus asked Peter three times—"Do you love Me?" Three times, Peter responded in the affirmative. Three times, Jesus gave instruction—"-Feed My lambs," "Tend My sheep," and "Feed my sheep" (Jn. 21:15–19).

> "Knowledge, benevolence, eloquence, gratitude, and zeal are all aids in the good work, but without the love of Jesus in the heart, the work of the Christian...is a failure."[68]

With a heart filled with love from God, inspiration from the Holy Spirit, and grace and thankfulness to Jesus for dying in our place, we can then go forward with energy, vigor, and excitement to share the gospel,

---

[68]White, *The Desire of Ages,* p. 815

the "good news" with our fellow man. What better way to enter into a relationship with God than to celebrate the day He set aside, rested upon, blessed, and made holy?

"In celebrating creation and salvation, remembering the Sabbath is the God-ordained practice of growing relationships between God and us—and then, through this ritual, between us and those around us."[69]

God's desire above all is to enter into a relationship with His creation. When He enters, He changes, He transforms, He renovates, He energizes us to draw us closer to Him and His love. Unless we have been transformed, we will have wasted our time of communion with God. We are fallen, broken, and sinful. God wants to change that situation. All the knowledge will not solve our condition. It is only His love indwelling within us can make us better, make us whole, make us holy as He has commanded us to be (1 Pet. 1:15–17).

Questions to Ponder:

What is my relationship today with God? Am I happy in my association with Him?

What do I need to change in my relationship with God?

Do I want to be changed?

Am I willing to allow God to make the necessary adjustments to my current condition in order that I might be drawn into a closer relationship with Him?

Take Away Notes:

---

[69] Brown, *For the Least of These*, p. 27

Divine Mercy, Divine Law—Perfect Fit

I n Exodus chapter 15, we find God healing the waters, so His children could drink. In Chapter 16, God provides manna for them to eat, as He taught them about His Sabbath rest. These people had been in bondage and now they were being given the opportunity to rest from their labors. Slaves were not given a day off. God, in His mercy, provides them that day of repose, relaxation, restfulness. In chapter 17, we read of the story of more water, this time, coming from the rock. There is a battle with the Amalekites, the first of many such battles, when much later in Israel's history, this nation is finally and utterly destroyed. Chapter 18 tells the story of Jethro, Moses' father-in-law, providing sound advice, good counsel, dealing with various levels of difficulty providing judgment. In each of these chapters, we detect the presence of God as He leads them to the mount where He will be meeting with them.

Finally, in chapter 19, the children of Israel arrive at Mount Sinai. While setting up their campsites around the base of the mount, Moses meets with God on this mount. God is now in the midst of these people, and God is preparing these people to begin to place their focus upon Him and His leading in their lives.

Exodus 19:4, *"You yourselves have seen what I did to the Egyptians, and how I bore you on eagles' wings and brought you to myself."* It has been about three months since their departure from Egypt. Before they departed from Egypt, they experienced the working of God on their behalf during the time of the plagues. They are now ready to consider worshiping this mighty God who has brought them to this place. God is willing to speak with the people. God is desiring to share with these people more amazing encounters with Himself.

God not only saw their affliction, He acted on their behalf. Exodus 20:1–2, *"And God spoke all these words, saying, 'I am the Lord your God, who brought you out of the land of Egypt, out of the house of slavery.'"* Because of His actions on their behalf, He set out basic laws which would be used by this new nation. They formed the basis of their constitution known as the Ten Commandments. These commandments were known by their ancestors back to Adam and Eve. Now, they are being reintroduced.

God is eager to begin establishing a relationship with these people. But they are frozen with fear. When they finally hear the voice of God speaking, they beg Moses for him to listen to God and they will listen to him, not God!

Try to imagine how God felt to be told no one wants to listen to Him speak! Yet God is gracious, He is loving, He is considerate. Isaiah 53:3–6 says:

*"He was **despised** and **rejected** by men;*

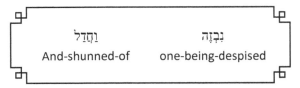

*A man of **sorrows** and acquainted with **grief**,*

And as one from whom men hide their faces
He was despised, and we esteemed Him not.
*Surely he has borne our **griefs***
*and carried our **sorrows**;*

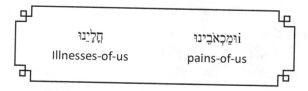

yet we esteemed him stricken,
smitten by God, and afflicted. But he was pierced for our
***transgressions**;*
*he was crushed for our **iniquities**;*

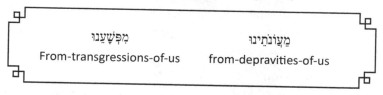

upon him was the chastisement that brought us peace,
and with his wounds we are healed.
All we like sheep have gone astray;
we have turned—every one—to his own way;
and the Lord has laid on him
the iniquity of us all." (Emphasis mine.)

Our condition is terminal. We are in pain, but we have numbed that pain, that illness with useless remedies, inept treatments, ineffective cures. Thus, we have an infection that will kill us, a sickness that will lead to death, unless we seek the Great Physician for His healing powers.

While we tend to recognize this passage to describe the coming Messiah, this passage also allows us to reflect upon the rejection God must have felt at the hands of the children of Israel. God bears not just the consequences of our sins (griefs and sorrows), He also bears the sins themselves (transgressions and iniquities). So, He turns to Moses and allows Moses to speak to the people. I wonder what the prime minister would say if the people asked me to speak to them, not the prime minister! This would never happen. But this did happen and to God Himself! No wonder Jesus sweat great drops of blood in Gethsemane (Lk. 22:44).

Between the giving of the constitution document, the Ten Commandments in chapter 20, and the building of the wilderness sanctuary (chapters 25–31), we find in chapters 21–23 laws about slaves, laws about restitution—dealing with personal injury and property protection; laws about social justice, and laws about the Sabbath and festivals.

The Ten Commandments deal with redemption while the sanctuary deals with recreation. Interestingly, the territory between deals with restoring inter-human relationships. "Bookended by the terrifying grandeur of the mountaintop and the purity and beauty of the sanctuary are surprisingly down-to-earth, practical, just and inclusive instructions for living well as God's people."[70]

Over the next several months, Moses climbs the mount to meet with God. As God rested upon Mount Sinai, God was demonstrating His desire to be in the midst of His people. God was revealing to them He was their rock, their protector, their sanctuary. Mount Sinai was the first tabernacle provided to the children of Israel.

Exodus 25:8, *"Let them make Me a sanctuary that I might dwell amongst them."* While God provided to the children of Israel a tabernacle (Mount Sinai), He had them build a tabernacle in which He could dwell. Through their own labor they would build this wilderness tabernacle, and thus they begin to see through their own handiwork, their own creation, God was willing to enter into their midst.

When working with children, especially those who have been traumatized, I will give them a project to do—drawing, painting, building blocks, etc.—and then through that project, I praise their efforts and

---

[70] Brown, *For the Least of These*, pp. 23–24

gently guide them into the next step of development. Through our interaction, we slowly, ever so slowly, begin the process of building a relationship. As this relationship develops, the child develops a foundation upon which they can anchor. God did the same with the children of Israel by allowing them to build the sanctuary to have a visual foundation upon which to rest, a base upon which to rely, a center for reconnecting.

Self-confidence can be a shaky foundation. Matthew 7:24–27 tells the story of the wise and foolish builders. The wise built his house upon the rock, the foolish on the sand. Jesus told His listeners two things were needed upon which to build on the rock: 1) hear the Word, and 2) obey the Word. While we may laud the individual who has self-confidence, we must realize from where this self-confidence comes.

God has given to each one unique talents, abilities, and skills. As we acknowledge God, we begin to be aware of God's presence. Seeing God's interaction in our lives provides security; experiencing God's presence in our life builds a confidence not only in oneself, but in the God who created you and me. Finally, to actually hear God speaking, whispering His love in our ear affirms our worth, confirms our own distinctiveness, establishes our position—being a daughter or son of God Himself.

God met with the children of Israel at Mount Sinai. There He provided Moses with the blueprints for the wilderness tabernacle. This tabernacle would travel with them over the next forty years. They may have been wearied, they may have suffered discouragement, they may have complained and grumbled, but the symbol of His presence was with them.

When Jesus came to earth, He set up His "tabernacle" in our midst. He dwelt in His "tent" by the side of the camps of men. He desired to dwell amongst us, He anticipated building a relationship with us, and He wanted us to become familiar with His and His Father's divine character and life. John 1:14, *"And the Word became flesh and dwelt among us, and we have seen his glory, glory as of the only [begotten] Son from the Father, full of grace and truth."* Jesus, the eternal God, took on human form so He could dwell with us, so He could "tabernacle" in our midst.

The Shekinah glory of the wilderness tabernacle was in Jesus while on earth. Jesus is greater than the wilderness tabernacle, greater than Solomon's temple, greater than Herod's temple present at the time Jesus dwelt upon this earth.

The main purpose for building this tabernacle was to have a visible presence for God right in the center of the encampment. It was also a visible center for all aspects of their living situations (civil, family, neighbor, health, and worship) as they traveled from place to place. It became a place of meeting for God and His creation. It became a living parable demonstrating God's plan to make humans whole—physically, spiritually, mentally.

As the wilderness sanctuary was situated in the center of the encampment, so today, God wishes to remain at the center of our lives. As we arise from our beds, our thoughts should turn to Him in praise for another night of sleep and another day of living in and for Him. As we go about our daily tasks, our thoughts should be centered upon Him, because, if our mind, our body, our strength are focused upon Him, our day will go much better for us. As we settle ourselves for the evening hours of quietude and relaxation, our thoughts must focus upon His guidance throughout the day and we are compelled to utter a word of thanks for His surety, His security, and His support. Finally, as we enter our beds, we utter our gratitude for allowing us to rest in His peace.

Offerings

Exodus 25:1, *"The Lord said to Moses, 'Tell the Israelites to bring me an offering. You are to receive the offering for me from everyone whose heart prompts them to give.'"*

"Devotion to God and a spirit of sacrifice were the first requisites in preparing a dwelling place for the Most High."[71]

---

[71]White, *Patriarchs and Prophets*, p. 343

This was a voluntary contribution to the construction of the desert tabernacle. We see the term "offering" in other passages, which can be voluntary or mandatory (Lev. 7:32–34). Offerings associated with sacrifices (Ex. 29:27), produce (Num. 16:19–21), or land (Ezk. 45) were voluntary. Offering with a census was mandatory (Ex. 30:11–16).

When the children of Israel left Egypt, they took the plunder with them. This plunder was the gold, the silver, the materials that would be needed for the construction of this wilderness tabernacle. They were asked for an offering and gave they did, so much so that Bezelal and Oholiab requested they stop giving (Ex. 31).

Ark of the Covenant

The Ark of the Covenant was the first piece to be described, detailed, and designed. It receives the first position, the first mention, and the first construction. It is with this piece, God becomes center of importance. This is where the Shekinah glory dwells.

Exodus 25:10–15, *"Have them make an ark of acacia wood— two and a half cubits long, a cubit and a half wide, and a cubit and a half high. Overlay it with pure gold, both inside and out, and make a gold molding around it. Cast four gold rings for it and fasten them to its four feet, with two rings on one side and two rings on the other. Then make poles of acacia wood and overlay them with gold. Insert the poles into the rings on the sides of the ark to carry it. The poles are to remain in the rings of this ark; they are not to be removed. Then put in the ark the tablets of the covenant law, which I will give you."*

"The Ark was not a statue meant to represent the physical manifestation of a god. It was not a container for God—it was to be respected but not worshiped. Instead, it was a place where God and man could meet. Both literally, as God would hover over the

Ark when the priests approached it, and figuratively through the law that was kept inside."[72]

a) Acacia Wood – *"Have them make an ark of acacia wood"* (Ex. 25:10 NIV).

Acacia wood is a type of wood that is derived from the acacia genus of trees and shrubs which are native to many areas of the world. There are more than a thousand different varieties of acacia tree. The hardwood that is derived from the tree is suitable for building long-lasting items of furniture and homewares. During the Israelites' journey through the wilderness, the acacia tree would be available and easily accessible.

Acacia (*atzei shittim* in Hebrew) was the only tree that grew in the desert in abundance and was more bush-like than tree-like.

Acacia wood is dense, thorny; the grain of the wood is gnarly (difficult, dangerous, and challenging) and changes direction.

It is resistant to decay, unpleasant to insects, thus, making an ideal building material that would be durable and long-lasting—the furniture in the wilderness was constantly being picked up and set down in a new location—and transportable as the Israelites sojourned and roamed in the desert.

The construction process was tricky as the wood could shatter if the tools used by the craftsmen were not kept sharp.

How We Are Like *Shittim* Wood

We are like the acacia wood—gnarly, our "grain" changing direction, thorny, not easy to work with. We can be very thick-headed and stiff-necked by times. But God loves to take gnarly things and cover them with gold, His gold, His character is the only gold we should seek.

---

[72] "What is significant about the Ark of the Covenant? What is it?" Compelling Truth, accessed February 9, 2020, https://www.compellingtruth.org/What-Ark-of-the-Covenant.html.

Today, we are God's dwelling place. When we consider how much care and concern God placed on this Ark, on this wilderness tabernacle, then we should not be surprised about how much He cares for us!

b) Pure Gold – Twenty-four karat gold is 100% pure gold and does not have other metal present; it is known as 99.9% pure. Twenty-two karat gold contains a little silver, zinc, or nickel and known as 91.67% pure. Eighteen karat gold contains 75% gold mixed with 25% other metals.

God wanted pure gold to cover the acacia wood. Pure gold comes the closest to describing the purity of God, the divinity of God. We will reveal our faith and love as we are tried in the fire. As gold becomes refined and pure in the fire, so we also will be made pure and refined in the fire of God's trials. Impurities cannot be removed without friction, without effort, without struggle. Therefore, we should not be surprised when trials, testing and tribulations come our way. God is purifying us, making us ready to dwell with Him forever in the kingdom He is preparing for our future habitation.

Durability of the Ark of the Covenant

Over the next 400 years, the Ark would have been used until it rested in the temple of Solomon. This includes the forty years of wandering in the desert, then 360 years, which included the era of the judges and covered the reigns of Saul, David, and Solomon. These three kings reigned a total of 120 years. When we read through the books of 1 and 2 Samuel, we note the Ark was constantly on the move.

Finally, the Ark was to remain in Solomon's temple until the Babylonian overthrow and destruction of the temple 345 years later. Where is the Ark now? No one knows. Many have searched and spent time and money trying to find this Ark, but still it remains hidden. Some conjecture the Ark was taken to heaven by God Himself. Others contend the Ark is located somewhere on this earth. While the Ark was needed at the time of the wilderness wanderings, we now have God's Word as our meeting place with God.

The Most Holy Place

The people were being commanded to place the most precious item in the world into this vessel they were to create. The very words of God carved into stone, by His own finger, were to be placed into an Ark made of acacia wood lined inside and out with gold.

The most holy place was the place where God met with His people. It was considered the most sacred place in the sanctuary. In it was the sacred Ark. What made it sacred, what made it holy? The presence of God.

Covering the Ark was the golden mercy seat with its two golden angels guarding over all. No acacia wood was used here. Between and above the cherubim was the cloudy pillar. It was the visible representation of God. Exodus 13:20–22, *"And they moved on from Succoth and encamped at Etham, on the edge of the wilderness. And the Lord went before them **by day in a pillar of cloud** to lead them along the way, and **by night in a pillar of fire** to give them light, that they might travel by day and by night. The pillar of cloud by day and the pillar of fire by night did not depart from before the people."* (Emphasis mine.)

Exodus 40:38, *"For the cloud of the Lord was on the tabernacle by day, and fire was in it by night, in the sight of all the house of Israel throughout all their journeys."*

But what does this mean for us who are alive today now? We who are awaiting the Second Coming of Jesus? For is it not the most holy place experience into which we must enter for us to join the heavenly family? In Hebrews 4:16, it says, *"Let us then with confidence draw near to the throne of grace, that we may receive mercy and find grace to help in time of need."* This is not a self-confidence identity entering before God, but a confidence **in** God and **for** God. A confidence that God is our Creator, our Father, our Redeemer. A confidence in His ability to keep us whole in Him, to make us one with Him.

Justification (complete forgiveness) was obtained in the outer court; **sanctification** (continuous victory over sin through obedience) is a lifetime of work in the holy place; and **glorification** (the complete character and image of Jesus Christ) within the most holy place in the presence of God Himself—these are the three steps from the altar of sacrifice to the throne of God. At the altar, He calls, "Come unto Me." From the throne, He calls, *"Come ye blessed of My Father, inherit the Kingdom prepared for you from the foundation of the world"* (Matt. 25:34).

Psalm 95:6–8:

> *"Oh come, let us worship and bow down;*
> *let us kneel before the Lord, our Maker!*
> **For he is our God,**
> **and we are the people of his pasture,**
> *and the sheep of his hand.*
> **Today, if you hear his voice,**
> **do not harden your hearts,** *as at Meribah,*
> *as on the day at Massah in the wilderness."* (Emphasis mine.)

"For He is our God, and we are the people of His pasture"—describes the covenant formula used by God in Exodus 6:7.

"Hardening one's heart is one of the worst choices one can make, because a person convinced about truth by the Holy Spirit but does not want to surrender and follow God's voice…. Such an attitude grieves God because in this case He cannot help. He respects our choice and decision."[73] While He respects our choice and decision, he allows us to reap the consequences, experience the results of our choice.

---

[73] Andrews Study Bible, notes on Psalm 95:8

Contents of the Ark of the Covenant

The Ark [Coffer] of the Covenant measured 3 ¾ ×2 ¼ ×2 ¼ feet and contained:

- Jar of Manna – Provisions

  Hebrews 9:4; Exodus 16:33–34: An *omer* was approximately two quarts. The pot of manna was to be a reminder of God's constant care for them during their wilderness journey. It is called Bread from Heaven. Jesus is the Bread of Life (Jn. 6:47–51, 58). He constantly cares for us physically, mentally, and spiritually.

- The Law – Ten Commandments – Standards for living

  Ten Commandments, called the Tables of Testimony (Ex. 32:15; Deut. 10:5). They were written on two tables of stone—both sides—with the finger of God, like a book. These commandments were the foundation of every aspect of daily living for the children of Israel, and they remain the foundation of every aspect of our daily living today.

- Aaron's Rod which budded – God's choice

  Aaron's rod that budded (Num. 17:10; Heb. 9:4). The almond tree was the first to blossom in the spring, and the Jewish people welcomed it. To them, it was a sign of new life; another spring had come. Numbers 16 and 17 tells of the rebellion of Korah, Dathan, and Abiram against Moses and Aaron. The rod was to be a sign against the rebels and remind them who God's chosen were. As God has given us power to choose, so He also has the power of choice.

The Ark was considered as God's dwelling place amongst His people. It symbolized His presence. Throughout their wanderings and settling into Canaan we can find several incidences where the Ark was utilized. Crossing the River Jordan, the Ark led the way. The Ark was a central presence at the walls of Jericho (Jos. 3:14–17; 6:6–21). **"Yet the ark could not be treated with irreverence because it was also a symbol of God's judgment and wrath."**[74] During the time of Samuel, Eli's two sons, Phinehas and Hophni took the ark out to the battlefield against the Philistines. They demonstrated a complete disregard to the commands of God and "summoned" God's presence. God allowed the Philistines to win the battle, He gave the Israelites over to their enemies, and "the glory departed from Israel, for the ark of the Lord was taken" (1 Sam. 4:22). God, in His mercy, confirmed His power, His might, His Strength, to the Philistines when Dagon, their god, was found fallen to the ground in the Ark's presence. After several Philistine cities were plagued, they returned the Ark to Israel (1 Sam. 5).

The Mercy Seat

Exodus 25:17 (NIV), *"Make an atonement cover [mercy seat] of pure gold—two and a half cubits long and a cubit and a half wide. And make two cherubim out of hammered gold at the ends of the cover"* ("mercy seat" ESV).

Was there any acacia used? No, only pure gold.

The mercy seat measured 3 ¾ × 2 ¼ feet. No thickness is recorded. Why? Could it be there is no measurement for the mercy of God?

But we must remember, there is a limit to the mercy of God. Or is there a limit? Revelation 21:6 tells us: *"And he said to me, 'It is done!*

---

[74]Bishop Darryl F. Husband Sr., DMin, *The Altared Life: The Pathway Towards Revival,* (Morrisville, NC: Lulu Press, 2008), p. 36.

[finished] I am the Alpha and the Omega, the beginning and the end. To the thirsty I will give from the spring of the water of life without payment. The one who conquers will have this heritage, and I will be his God and he will be my son.'"

Three times we find the word "finished" or "completed" in the Bible.

First time we find it in Genesis 2:2—where God has finished the work of His Creation.

Second time we find it in John 19:30—where Jesus says, "It is *finished*," meaning that, "It has been paid in full," "The debt is no more."

When Christ died on the cross, He broadcast His dramatic statement, "It is *finished*." Justice and mercy were satisfied, Satan's charges were refuted, and humanity was set free.[75]

Third and last time it is found in Revelation 16:17—where from out of the temple, came a loud voice saying "It is *finished*," meaning evil no longer has a chance against God.[76]

Even as we consider the final outcome for the wicked, God is still merciful. When they are destroyed—not burning in hell, but completely and utterly reduced to ashes—God is demonstrating His mercy. He does not want to torture these people throughout eternity.

Divine Mercy fits the divine law precisely, and together, they highlight the two main elements of the divine character—justice and mercy. As Jesus was hanging on the cross, paying the price of justice, the thief asked Jesus to remember him in His kingdom. The thief was asking for mercy in the midst of God's justice. Luke 23:39–43 *"One of the criminals who were hanged railed at him, saying, 'Are you not the Christ? Save yourself and us!' But the other rebuked him, saying, 'Do you not fear*

---

[75] Blake, *Searching For a God to Love,* p. 254

[76] Mano Paul, "It Is Finished—Genesis to Revelation," Hidden Treasures, March 7, 2009, accessed February 9, 2020, https://thepauls.wordpress.com/2009/03/07/it-is-finished-genesis-to-revelation/.

God, since you are under the same sentence of condemnation? And we indeed justly, for we are receiving the due reward of our deeds; but this man has done nothing wrong.' And he said, 'Jesus, remember me when you come into your kingdom.' And he said to him, 'Truly, I say to you today, you will be with me in paradise.'"

Our self-confidence, our strength is anchored in God's grace and His joy over our salvation and commitment. Jesus hints at that when He says there is more joy in heaven over even one sinner who repents (Lk. 15:7).[77] We can believe God is our Creator, our Redeemer. We can live a life we know we should be living. We fail miserably. Unless God's mercy covers His Divine law, we will not be saved.

Questions to Ponder:

Is there something I must do to prepare my body to be inhabited by God?

Am I living a life wherein others know God is dwelling within me?

Am I demonstrating God's tender mercy all the while I am living God's life of justice?

Do I extend mercy and grace to others who seek these from me?

Take Away Notes:

---

[77] Gerald A. Klingbeil, "The Joy of the Lord Is Your Strength," *Adventist Journey,* Vol. 2, No. 6, June 2019.

DIVINE PRESENCE, DIVINE SUSTENANCE

Exodus 25:30; 33:13–14; 40:34–38: *"And you shall set the bread of the Presence on the table before me regularly"* (ESV). *"And you shall set the showbread on the table before Me always"* (NKJV). Literally, *"the bread of faces."* It represents divine presence and divine sustenance.

Exodus 33:13–14, *"'Now therefore, if I have found favor in your sight, please show me now your ways, that I may know you in order to find favor in your sight. Consider too that this nation is your people.' And he said, 'My presence will go with you, and I will give you rest.'"*

Exodus 40:34–38, *"Then the cloud covered the tent of meeting, and the glory of the Lord filled the tabernacle. And Moses was not able to enter the tent of meeting because the cloud settled on it, and the glory of the Lord filled the tabernacle. Throughout all their journeys, whenever the cloud was taken up from over the tabernacle, the people of Israel would set out. But if the cloud was not taken up, then they did not set out till the day that it was taken up. For the cloud of the Lord was on the tabernacle by day, and fire was in it by night, in the sight of all the house of Israel throughout all their journeys."*

The Bread of the Presence – Divine Presence

פָּנִים   לֶחֶם

Faces   bread-of

The bread was placed on the table every week. This was one more reminder to the people of God's presence. God has elected to dwell amongst His creation. Today we participate in the communion service, we have the bread, this time broken, to remind us of Jesus' sacrifice for us. This communion service prompts us to remember He has redeemed us to Himself, to demonstrate His presence with us today and His willingness to remain near and in each one.

As with the Ark of the Covenant, this table was also mobile. Jesus moves about and around us, sharing His love with us, providing us His presence and His sustenance.

God Calls Moses

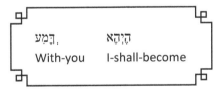

הֶמָּע,   הֶיֶה א

With-you   I-shall-become

Exodus 3:12, *"He said, 'But I will be with you, and this shall be the sign for you, that I have sent you: when you have brought the people out of Egypt, you shall serve God on this mountain.'"* Moses was at the burning bush. God has been telling him about the mission He is about to send Moses on. This is in response to Moses' question: "Who am I, that I should go before Pharaoh?" Moses is very much afraid to go before Pharaoh. There is no statute of limitations for murder. God repeats His promise to be with Moses after his fourth objection. Reminding Moses, He is the Creator, God again tells Moses, *"Now therefore go, and I will be with your mouth and teach you what you shall speak"* (Ex. 4:12).

As God told Moses on the mount, Jesus told His disciples (you and me) in Matthew 10:19–20, *"When they deliver you over, do not be anxious how you are to speak or what you are to say, for what you are to say will be given to you in that hour. For it is not you who speak, but the Spirit of your Father speaking through you."*

As with Moses, so God had been with Jacob when He told him to return to the land of his fathers—He would be with him. Genesis 31:3, *"Then the Lord said to Jacob, 'Return to the land of your fathers and to your kindred, and I will be with you.'"* To "become" indicates to convert, to turn into, to grow into, to come to be. This means more than just walking side by side, holding hands, or linking arms. This is God entering into our being, sharing the most intimate thoughts, the deepest emotions, becoming one with our Creator. Being one with God is not becoming God ourselves, but allowing God to handle, take charge, and deal with all the issues we face day by day.

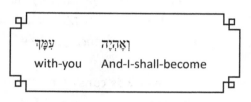

עִמָּךְ   וְאֶהְיֶה
with-you   And-I-shall-become

Seeking God's Presence

Have you ever found yourself seeking God's presence only to realize God is already present? On several occasions, I have found myself in a crowd searching for a certain individual; when our eyes finally focus upon each other, we immediately respond with relief, happiness, and contentment that the search is over. All of a sudden, we stand straighter, walk taller, run or walk faster toward each other, and generally become more aware of who each is, what we are doing, and checking our surroundings to determine a faster, shorter, route in order to reach each other. This is how we should be seeking God in our day-to-day adventures, excursions.

Exodus 33:13–14, *"Now therefore, if I have found favor in your sight, **please show me now your ways,** that I may know you in order to find favor in your sight. Consider too that this nation is your people. And he* *said, 'My presence [פָּנַי faces-of-me] will go with you, and I will give you rest.'"* God had given the command to leave Mount Sinai. He had stated He Himself would not go with them, but He would send an angel to accompany them. He would uphold His promise to bring the children of Israel to Canaan, but not by Himself directly. The Israelites were stiff-necked. Because of Moses' intercession, God relented and promised Moses, *"My presence [פָּנַי faces-of-me] will go with you, and I will give you rest."*

Moses was considered the meekest of men. Yet he asked God to "show me now your ways." The more we know God, the more we realize we do not know Him, and we desire to better understand His character and plans in order to walk in His truth.[78] This can only happen if we are sincere, have a teachable heart, and a commitment to fully surrender our all to Him.

Isaiah's Prayer

Isaiah 63:9, *"In all their affliction he was afflicted, and the Angel of his Presence [פָּנָיו – faces-of-him] saved them; in his love and in his pity, he redeemed them; he lifted them up and carried them all the days of old."* This is part of the prayer of Isaiah recounting the mercy of God, similar to Daniel as he prayed in Daniel 9, recounting God's covenant relationship with His people. Verses 17b–18, we read: *"O Lord, make your face to shine upon your sanctuary, which is desolate. O my God incline your ear and hear. Open your eyes and see our desolations, and the city that is called by your name. For we do not present our pleas before you because of our righteousness, but because of your great mercy."* God remembers His part in the covenant, we, His children, tend to forget and so we look to other means to order our lives. We rely upon our day timers, our alarm clocks, our work, our relations with our fellow humans, our computers, our habits, the list goes on and on. How much easier it would be if we learned and remembered to lean upon our

---

[78]Andrews Study Bible, note Psalm 86:11

Father. To embrace the character of God is to become His children. Adopted as we are, God still pours His mercy upon us and fills us with His love, His joy, His peace, His forgiveness, His life.

When Moses inaugurated Joshua to the head of Israel, He repeats that God would be with him in his leadership. (Deuteronomy 31:23, *"And the Lord commissioned Joshua the son of Nun and said, 'Be **strong** and **courageous**, for you shall bring the people of Israel into the land that I swore to give them. I will be with you.'"* [Emphasis mine.])

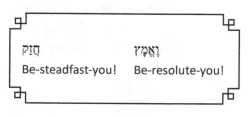

God Himself repeats this same promise to Joshua in Joshua 1:5. Joshua was told to be strong and courageous and God would be with him. Strong's Concordance suggests for "strong"—to fasten up, to seize, take hold, withstand, conquer;[79] and for "courageous"—a primitive root; to be alert, physically (on foot) or mentally (in courage) steadfastly mindful.[80]

Also, we must remember Jesus' own promise to us, His disciples. Matthew 28:20, *"teaching them to observe all that I have commanded you. And behold, I **am with you** always, to the end of the age."* (Emphasis mine.)

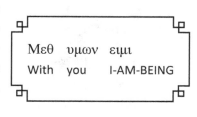

While we translate both the Hebrew and Greek as "I am with you," I would submit it is more than "with you." First John 2:5–6 says, *"whoever*

---

[79] "Strong's Definitions," Blue Letter Bible, accessed February 9, 2020, https://www. blueletterbible.org/lang/Lexicon/Lexicon.cfm?strongs=H2388&t=KJV.

[80] Ibid.

keeps his word, in him truly the love of God is perfected. By this we may know that we are in him: whoever says he abides in him ought to walk in the same way in which he walked." God wants to abide in us and He also wants us to abide in Him. Thus, while He promises to be with us, He is essentially saying "abiding" in each other. In other words, remaining in a close, continuous, intimate, personal relationship with Him. When we become this close, we will only do and say what God is saying and doing.

I recall a program in which a traumatized child was rescued by his benefactor. He did not want to be near anyone else except for the one who rescued him. Thus, for a time, he lived in his rescuer's home, copied his every move, dressed as he dressed, ate what he ate. There was one thing he could not copy—his champion did not require sleep. While he tried mightily, he failed miserably. He concluded he would never become exactly like his rescuer.

We need also to come to this realization. While we can copy our heavenly Father, obey His every command, behave as He does, speak the words He speaks, we will never be able to be GOD. That is okay. That is correct. That is the way it should remain. This does not negate the close, personal relationship, the connection, the bond both God and His own children (you and I who have chosen Him) desire.

Cloud by Day, Pillar of Fire by Night

Exodus 40:34–38, *"Then the cloud covered the tent of meeting, and the glory of the Lord filled the tabernacle. And Moses was not able to enter the tent of meeting because the cloud settled on it, and the glory of the Lord filled the tabernacle. Throughout all their journeys, whenever the cloud was taken up from over the tabernacle, the people of Israel would set out. But if the cloud was not taken up, then they did not set out till the day that it was taken up. For the cloud of the Lord was on the tabernacle by day, and fire was in it by night, in the sight of all the house of Israel throughout all their journeys."*

"'As the Lord had commanded, even so had they done it: and Moses blessed them.' With eager interest, the multitudes of Israel crowded around to look upon the sacred structure. While they were contemplating the scene with reverent satisfaction, the pillar of cloud floated over the sanctuary and, descending, enveloped it. 'And the glory of the Lord filled the tabernacle.' There was a revealing of the divine majesty, and for a time even Moses could not enter. With deep emotion, the people beheld the token that the work of their hands was accepted. There were no loud demonstrations of rejoicing. A solemn awe rested upon all. But the gladness of their hearts welled up in tears of joy, and they murmured low, earnest words of gratitude that God had condescended to abide with them."[81]

Questions to Ponder:

Have I allowed God to enter me?

Have I entered into the presence of God?

Does my life demonstrate this interaction?

Take Away Notes:

---

[81] White, *Patriarchs and Prophets*, p. 349

PART TWO:
DIVINE SUSTENANCE

Exodus 25:30 (NKJV), *"And you shall set the bread of the Presence on the table before me regularly."* *"And you shall set the show-bread on the table before Me always."* Literally, *"the bread of faces."* It represents divine presence and sustenance.

Before the construction of the table of gold with the bread of the *presence*, the showbread, God was already providing physical food for the children of Israel—manna. We find this story in Exodus 16. On the fifteenth day of the second month, before they have arrived at Mount Sinai, they are grumbling, complaining about lack of food. While the food situation was not at a crisis stage, the complaints were ongoing. In their imaginings, they saw themselves and their children starving.

They could not trust God to supply their needs. Even with the recent events of the plagues, the Passover meal, the departure from Egypt, the crossing of the Red Sea, and God healing the bitter water, they were sure they would die of hunger. God needed them to endure some hardships, to help them turn to Him for their basic needs. This, they could not bring themselves to do.

"God was bringing them from a state of degradation and fitting them to occupy an honorable place among the nations and to receive important and sacred trusts."[82]

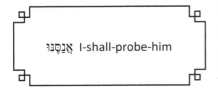
אֲנַסֶּנּוּ I-shall-probe-him

Exodus 16:4, *"Then the Lord said to Moses, 'Behold, I am about to rain bread from heaven for you, and the people shall go out and gather a day's*

---

[82] White, Patriarchs and Prophets, p. 292

portion every day, that I may test them, whether they will walk in my law or not.'"

To probe, to investigate, God understands us better than we comprehend ourselves. Moses told the Israelites God was going to provide them bread from heaven in order to test them. Would they obey His Word, His commands?

Psalm 139:23–24, **"Search me, O God, and know my heart! Try me and know my thoughts! [cares] And see if there be any grievous way in me and lead me in the way everlasting!"** (Emphasis mine.) David is asking God to probe, to investigate his

חָקְרֵנִי   investigate-you-me!

heart, his mind, his soul, his motives. He is asking God to make whatever changes necessary, so he could stand in holiness before His God. This needs to be our prayer today. God knows us better than we do ourselves.

Providing Bread

Psalm 23:5, *"You prepare a table before me in the presence of my enemies."* As the shepherd enters a pasture with his sheep, his eyes are on the lookout for any dangers. Once he has ascertained the safety of the area, he then prepares the place where the sheep can eat in peace, rest in security, and congregate in ease. Oh, that we could learn to trust God as sheep trust their shepherd.

For several years, I raised goats. Starting with two pregnant females, I eventually had upwards to thirty-six goats—males and females, adults and young. Each displayed their own unique characteristics. My relationship with them was one of trust and love. They knew me and knew just how far they could go with me. They followed me everywhere I went. They were not happy being out of my sight unless they were in their pens in the barn. They willingly went into their pens, because they knew I had prepared their bedding and feeding areas. Psalm 23 took on new understanding for me as I tended these goats. I began to realize God does the same with me. We can trust God "to prepare our tables."

Eating the Bread

Psalm 34:8, *"Oh, taste and see that the Lord is good! Blessed is the man who takes refuge in him!"* Taste and see—two words which describes two of the five senses man has. How do we then taste? We might better understand the seeing element easier, but David is telling us to do both—taste and see.

"Taste" can be described as savor, discriminate, distinguish; while "see" can be described as comprehend, realize, appreciate.

How do we "taste and see" that the Lord is good? Before tasting anything, we must eat something. Before eating something, we must "see" the food. From the beginning, God gave man food to see and to eat (taste).

Genesis 2:9, *"And out of the ground the Lord God made every tree grow that is pleasant to the sight and good for food."*

"Adam was created with a natural hunger for food, so God gave him the produce of the Garden to satisfy his hunger. God also created Adam with a spiritual hunger that only **He** could satisfy through an intimate relationship that included direct communication (God spoke directly to Adam)."[83]

Do we still hunger and thirst today? Of course, both physically and spiritually. Matthew 5:6, *"Blessed are those who hunger and thirst for righteousness, for they shall be satisfied."* Only through communion

---

[83] Shari Abbott, "What Does It Mean to Taste and See That God Is Good? (Psalm 34)," Reasons for Hope* Jesus, August 18, 2018, accessed February 9, 2020, https://reasonsforhopejesus.com/taste-and-see/.

with God can we be satisfied. But this satisfaction will not last unless we continue in community with Him—our Creator, our Redeemer, our Father.

God instilled in us a hunger for His Word. He knows His Word nourishes our souls; therefore, when we hunger, we are to cry out in desire and in need for the pure Word and faithful teachings so that we will grow spiritually, and we will "taste and see" the goodness and grace of our God.

First Peter 2:2–3, *"as newborn babes, desire the pure milk of the word, that you may grow thereby, if indeed you have tasted that the Lord is gracious."* It is the WORD of God which provides the nourishment which will help us to grow spiritually. God could have destroyed us from the very beginning when our first parents fell, but God demonstrates His graciousness by feeding us the food fit for our growth. Therefore, the more we eat, the more we grow; the more we grow, the more we develop into the creation God planned from the beginning.

Psalm 119:103, *"How sweet are Your words to **my taste**,*
Sweeter than honey to my mouth!"
Psalm 19: 7–10 7, *"The law of the Lord is **perfect**,*
[blameless] reviving the soul;
*the testimony of the Lord is **sure**, making wise the simple;*
*the precepts of the Lord are **right**, rejoicing the heart;*
*the commandment of the Lord is **pure**, enlightening the eyes;*
*the fear of the Lord is **clean**, enduring forever;*
*the rules [decrees] of the Lord are **true**, and **righteous altogether**.*
More to be desired are they than gold, even much fine gold;
***sweeter also than honey and drippings of the honeycomb**."*
(Emphasis mine.)

When God reveals Himself to us, we develop a greater desire to taste more, to glean more, to absorb more. We are drawn closer and nearer to Him as His love within us grows and matures.

169

"Without the law, men have no just conception of the purity and holiness of God or of their own guilt and uncleanness. They have no true conviction of sin and feel no need of repentance. Not seeing their lost condition as violators of God's law, they do not realize their need of the atoning blood of Christ. The hope of salvation is accepted without a radical change of heart or reformation of life. Thus, superficial conversions abound, and multitudes are joined to the church who have never been united to Christ."[84]

Thus, it is not knowledge we are seeking, but a relationship with our Creator, a communion with our Redeemer, a connection (which sin severed) with our Father.

Jar of Manna

When we consider the Ark of the Covenant, we note one of the items inserted was the container of manna. God provided the physical manna for the Israelites to demonstrate His divine sustenance. For forty years God provided them with physical food from heaven.

- Jar of Manna – Provisions

  Hebrews 9:4; Exodus 16:33–34: An *omer* was approximately two quarts. The pot of manna was to be a reminder of God's constant care for them during their wilderness journey, a vivid reminder of past divine leading.

  It is called Bread from Heaven. Jesus is the Bread of Life John 6:47–51, 58. He constantly cares for us physically, mentally, and spiritually.

---

[84] White, *The Great Controversy Between Christ and Satan*, p. 468

Jesus' use of "I AM" were used in three ways:

1) Simple self-identification at a human level (John 6:20 – It is I, literally I AM).
2) Use of metaphors to point to the spiritual life Jesus offers (Bread of Life, the Light, the Door, the Good Shepherd; the Way, the Truth, and the Life; the True Vine, the Resurrection and the Life).
3) As a direct claim to deity (Jn. 8:28, 58; 13:19).

Jesus as the "Bread of Life" (Jn. 6:35–50) also is making a reference to the Lord's Supper (verses 50–59). This Jesus is the "Bread" that leads to eternal life (17:3)—available through a relationship with Jesus. Thus, it is not solely knowledge we are seeking, but a relationship with our Creator, a communion with our Redeemer, a connection (which sin severed) with our Father.

Questions to Ponder:

Am I tasting nourishing food in my study of God's WORD?

Do I sense a desire to know my Creator more today than I did yesterday?

Take Away Notes:

Divine Glory, Divine Beauty

Exodus 28:1–2, *"Then bring near to you Aaron your brother, and his sons with him, from among the people of Israel, **to serve me as priests**—Aaron and Aaron's sons, Nadab and Abihu, Eleazar and Ithamar. And you shall make holy garments for Aaron your brother, **for glory** and **for beauty**."* (Emphasis mine.)

Ministering to the Lord

"The priestly garments had a signal, [a marked] function and denoted the occupation of Aaron and his sons as closely associated with the tabernacle. They

offered sacrificial offerings and gifts and served as teachers of the law, constantly reminding the people of their covenant obligations to God (Deut. 31:9–13; Neh. 8:2–3; Jer. 18:18)."[85]

Every seven years, the Israelites were to be freed from their debt from each other. At the Feast of Tabernacles, their harvest would be completed. With these two major concerns gone, this would be a good time to present to them the law, so they could renew their commitment to keeping the law and their covenant with God.

---

[85] Andrews Study Bible, notes for Exodus 28:1–4

"Had this counsel been heeded through the centuries that followed, how different would have been Israel's history!"[86]

Jeremiah's Dilemma

Jeremiah 18:18, *"Then they said, 'Come, let us make plots against Jeremiah, for the law shall not perish from the priest, nor counsel from the wise, nor the word from the prophet. Come, let us strike him with the tongue, and let us not pay attention to any of his words.'"*

Jeremiah's opponents believed God spoke through their own leaders and rejected his messages. Often, this occurs when we forget the basics of our beliefs. Unless we study God's Word diligently, we will begin to believe others who offer soothing words, or tickling words.

Recently, I asked twenty questions concerning the celebration of Christmas. Two small groups of members were asked these questions. As Christians, we pride ourselves on celebrating "Christmas" having taken the pagan holiday of the solstice and making it "Christian" holiday. Both barely passed the 50% of the answers. We began to realize we have been taking the traditions of past generations, not the Word of God.

Proverbs 26:23–26 says, *"Like the glaze [silver of dross] covering an earthen vessel are fervent lips with an evil heart. Whoever hates disguises himself with his lips and harbors deceit in his heart; when he speaks graciously, believe him not, for there are seven abominations in his heart; though his hatred be covered with deception, his wickedness will be exposed in the assembly."* Jesus stated that Satan is known as the "father of lies" (Jn. 8:44). His lies have permeated in society, and today, we are reaping the results—we must ever remember to be "politically correct" in our speech; we compromise our

---

[86] White, *Prophets and Kings*, p. 465

God-required law with everyone we encounter so as not to offend their own values; and we acknowledge open sin despite knowing God's Word.

Second Timothy 2:15 (KJV), *"Study to shew thyself approved unto God, a workman that needeth not to be ashamed, **rightly dividing** the word of truth."* "*Do your best to present yourself to God as one approved, a worker who has no need to be ashamed, **rightly handling** the word of truth"* (ESV).

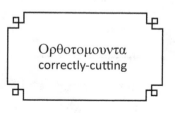

Ορθοτομουντα
correctly-cutting

Too little do we review the foundational elements of our beliefs today. Unless the basics of our lives are reviewed and renewed, decay, destruction, decline, deterioration, degeneration occurs.

The priests and the elders had the responsibility to ensure the law was made known to the people, the covenant obligations were treated, maintained and taught to the members of their nation, so they could not only obey these laws but also put into effect God's instructions.

Understanding

Nehemiah 8:2–3, *"So Ezra the priest brought the Law before the assembly, both men and women and all who could understand what they heard, on the first day of the seventh month. And he read from it facing the square before the Water Gate from early morning until midday, in the presence of the men and the women and those who could understand. And the ears of all the people were attentive to the Book of the Law."*

The term "understand" is used six times in this chapter. "[This] term is often used in wisdom literature and suggests not only intellectual knowledge, but the ability to wisely understand (and apply) moral choices."[87]

מֵבִין one-understanding using-intelligence (1 Chron. 15:22; considering Dan. 8:5)

It is intriguing to note also the order of the people attending—"both men and women and all who could understand what they heard." There were men and women present who could NOT understand. When one encounters an individual who does not understand, greater effort is needed to ensure this understanding, perception, discerning takes place.

> Exodus 28:3–4, *"You shall speak to all the skillful, whom I have filled with a spirit of skill, that they make Aaron's garments to consecrate him for my priesthood. These are the garments that they shall make: a breastpiece, an ephod, a robe, a coat of checker work, a turban, and a sash. They shall make holy garments for Aaron your brother and his sons to serve me as priests."*

In verse one above, God instructed these garments to be made so Aaron and his sons could "serve [God] as priests. **Aaron and his sons were not consecrated to minister unto man, but unto the Lord on behalf of man.**[88] (Emphasis mine.)

For Beauty

"In the beginning God created the heavens and the earth" (Gen. 1:1). Even while God created the earth and mankind, He shared His beauty with us. He could have provided the basics of living conditions, but He

---

[87] Andrews Study Bible, notes for Nehemiah 8:2–3

[88] "Glory and Beauty," Grace Baptist Huntsville, accessed February 9, 2020, http://www.gracebaptisthuntsville.org/share/gloryandbeauty.htm.

created beauty instead. Color, texture, smells, sight, taste, sounds were all incorporated in the creating process. As God enjoys fully His universe, so He made it for our enjoyment as well. He proclaimed His masterpiece as "very good" (Gen. 1:31).

Charles Darwin once wrote that the sight of a male peacock's tail made him physically ill. Why? He knew that the unnecessary beauty so prevailing throughout the living world points unquestionably to intelligent design, knowledgeable foresight and higher plan (Isa. 55:9). When we explore the creativity and stunning effects of regular colors, arrangement of logical and perfect patterns, and adornment in the animal and plant kingdoms that exist for a purpose beyond mere survival.

"These are the garments that they shall make: a breastpiece, an ephod, a robe, a coat of checker work, a turban, and a sash. They shall make holy garments for Aaron your brother and his sons to serve me as priests. They shall receive gold, blue and purple and scarlet yarns, and fine twined linen" (Ex. 28:4–5). God could have commanded only a dark suit, white shirt, with black tie and shoes, but God loves color, patterns, brilliance, and texture.

The Ark of the Covenant was made of two pieces—the box which contained the testimony of God and the mercy seat covering. Intricate molding and crafting were put into this piece of furniture. Throughout the years, men have attempted to find this ark. It disappeared at the time of Jerusalem's fall to the Babylonians. Solomon's temple was destroyed, the gold, silver, and other precious metals and stones were taken, but not the Ark of the Covenant.

The breastplate and ephod of the high priest also are two components. The ephod contained the two onyx stones which rested upon the shoulders. The shoulder stones were for remembrance before God. The breast piece was over the heart for judgment. Both were attached together.

While the Ark of the Covenant was considered the most important item in the tabernacle, the breastplate was considered the most important piece of Aaron's clothing. Detail was put into the creating of this breastplate.

The gold, blue, purple, scarlet, and fine twined linen will be discussed fully in the next chapter, "Divine Consent and Divine Denial." For now, we need to acknowledge God had a reason for using these colors and elements.

Gold—represents God's divinity. Psalm 19:7–10, *"The law of the Lord is perfect...the testimony of the Lord is sure...the precepts of the Lord are right...the commandment of the Lord is pure...the fear of the Lord is clean...the rules of the Lord are true...more to be desire are they than gold."* We reveal our faith, our love, our commitment as we are tried in the fire. Like gold being refined in the fire, so we also must be refined in the fire of God's trials. Impurities cannot be removed without friction, without effort, without struggle.

Blue—represents the divine law—God's law. Numbers 15:37–41, *"The Lord said to Moses, 'Speak to the people of Israel, and tell them to make tassels on the corners of their garments throughout their generations, and to put a cord of blue on the tassel of each corner. And it shall be a tassel for you to look at and remember all the commandments of the Lord, to do them, not to follow after your own heart and your own eyes, which you are inclined to whore after. So you shall remember and do all my commandments and be holy to your God. I am the Lord your God, who brought you out of the land of Egypt to be your God: I am the Lord your God.'"*

Purple—represents divine royalty—His kingdom. John 19:2–3, *"And the soldiers twisted together a crown of thorns and put it on his head and arrayed him in a purple robe. They came up to him, saying, 'Hail, King of the Jews!' and struck him with their hands."* Though these soldiers were mocking Jesus, we understand even pagan nations recognize purple for royalty.

Scarlet—symbolizes the service and sacrifice of Jesus. Hebrews 9:22, *"Indeed, under the law almost everything is purified with blood, and without the shedding of blood there is no forgiveness of sins."*

Fine twined linen—refers to the purity of Jesus Himself—His righteousness, His truth. First Peter 1:8–9 *"Though you have not seen him, you love him. Though you do not now see him, you believe in him and rejoice with joy that is inexpressible and filled with glory, obtaining the outcome of your faith, the salvation of your souls."*

Breastplate

While the breastplate was embedded with beautiful and special stones, and the names of each tribe was inscribed on these stones, we must acknowledge there is no mention of an order of which tribe is listed and where. Some scholars have attempted to list a given tribe with a given stone. Scripture does not so indicate.

What stones were placed in this breastplate? According to Exodus 28:17–21: *"You shall set in it four rows of stones. A row of sardius, topaz, and carbuncle shall be the first row; and the second row an emerald, a sapphire, and a diamond; and the third row a jacinth, an agate, and an amethyst; and the fourth row a beryl, an onyx, and a jasper. They shall be set in gold filigree."*

"We consider these precious stones placed within the breastplate, we are intrigued by the beauty, we are awed that God desired to use these gems; but we should remember they all came from clay or sand. [God] did not transform what was already rare and precious. But He took what man too often despises to produce His masterpieces. Each dirt-born precious stone echoes the words of our Lord, 'I came not to call the righteous, but the sinners to repentance' (Mk. 2:17).... Their genesis is a parable of Jehovah's method of dealing with humanity. At creation He added His breath to a human figure shaped out of dust and a child of God came into being."[89]

As each tribe was listed on these stones and placed over the heart of Aaron, today, we stand before God as Jesus bears us upon His heart. When we accept Jesus as our Savior, we are born of the Spirit of God, saved by grace, and receive the unmerited favor of God.

When we stand before the cross of Christ, we are all on even ground. No one is more important to God till the moment that individual comes with a contrite and committed heart before the cross.

The Glory of the Lord

> Exodus 40:34, *"Then the cloud covered the tent of meeting, and the glory of the Lord filled the tabernacle."*

The glory of the LORD fills this tabernacle, and 500 years later, fills the temple of Solomon.

> First Kings 8:10–11, *"And when the priests came out of the Holy Place, a cloud filled the house of the Lord, so that the priests could not stand to minister because of the cloud, for the glory of the Lord filled the house of the Lord."*

> Second Chronicles 5:5, 13–14: *"Then the priests brought the ark of the covenant of the Lord to its place, in the inner sanctuary of the house, in the Most Holy Place, underneath the wings of the cherubim...and it was the duty of the trumpeters and singers to make themselves heard in unison in praise and thanksgiving to the Lord), and when the song was raised, with trumpets and cymbals and other musical instruments, in praise to the Lord,*

---

[89] Leslie Hardinge, *Ambassadors: Studies on the 13 Apostles*, (Hagerstown, MD: Review and Herald Publishing Association, 2004), pp. 13–14.

'For he is good, for his steadfast love endures forever, the house, the house of the Lord, was filled with a cloud, so that the priests could not stand to minister because of the cloud, for the glory of the Lord filled the house of God.'"

Forty years earlier, King David had brought the Ark into Jerusalem. Now that Solomon had built the temple, the Ark can now find its resting place. When the glory of the Lord filled this temple, God indicated the holiness of the sanctuary.

Mark 11 tells the story of Jesus riding on the colt, coming into Jerusalem and into the temple. Verse 11, *"And he entered Jerusalem and went into the temple. And when he had looked around at everything, as it was already late, he went out to Bethany with the twelve."* The next morning, Jesus returns and casts out the temple merchants stating, *"Is it not written, 'My house shall be called a house of prayer for all the nations'? But you have made it a den of robbers"* (verse 17). The chief priests and scribes, instead of accepting Jesus' rebuke, sought means to destroy Him. The glory of the Lord was present in that temple, but the priests did not recognize this. Instead of acknowledging the glory of the Lord's presence, they challenged Him, they disputed with Him, they doubted Him, they killed Him.

Isaiah 1:16–18:

"Wash yourselves; make yourselves clean;
remove the evil of your deeds from before my eyes;
cease to do evil..."

Ceremonial washing without giving up evil deeds and committing to justice avails nothing and consist of religious hypocrisy.[90]

---

[90] Andrews Study Bible, note Isaiah 1:16

"learn to do good;
seek justice,
correct oppression;
bring justice to the fatherless,
plead the widow's cause."

The basic intent of the covenant is justice or fairness to all people and the respect of the rights of all people.[91]

"Come now, let us reason together, says the Lord:
though your sins are like scarlet,
they shall be as white as snow;
though they are red like crimson,
they shall become like wool."

God is demonstrating His intent to work with each one on an individual basis to bring each to Himself. He is desiring to make us free from the bondage of sin, to live a life in abundance of His love, His joy, His truth. Our part is to submit wholly, completely, no reservation to His amazing care, protection, covered in His righteousness to live a life of holiness.

In the first chapter, Moses confronted the burning bush—a bush that did not burn. He heard his name called, but was told not to draw near, took off his sandals for the ground was holy. What was it made the ground holy? Only ONE makes the ground holy. Only ONE makes anything and anyone holy. That ONE is not wholly man, but wholly GOD.

Solomon's temple—2 Chronicles 5:13b–14, *"when the song was raised, with trumpets and cymbals and other musical instruments, in praise to the Lord, 'For he is good, for his steadfast love endures forever,' the house, the house of the Lord, was filled with a cloud, so that the priests could not stand to minister because of the cloud, for the glory of the Lord filled the house of God."*

---

[91] Ibid., Isaiah 1:17

The temple has been built and now the Israelites are dedicating this temple to the name of their God. God accepts their sacrifices and consumes them with His own fire and fills the temple with His own glory. The priests must move out of the temple because of the cloud of His glory.

Second Chronicles 7:3, *"When all the Israelites saw the fire coming down and the glory of the Lord above the temple, they knelt on the pavement with their faces to the ground, and they worshiped and gave thanks to the Lord, saying, 'He is good; his love endures forever.'"*

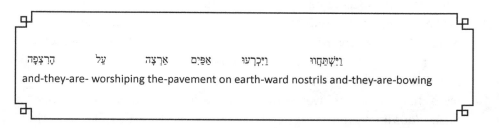

הָרִצְפָה   עַל   אַרְצָה אַפַּיִם   וַיִּכְרְעוּ   וַיִּשְׁתַּחֲווּ

and-they-are- worshiping the-pavement on earth-ward nostrils and-they-are-bowing

Worship is the response when seeing the glory of God. We are compelled to raise our voices in praise to give honor to the ONE who willingly interweaves in our lives, who desires to have us as His own, who loves us with an everlasting love, so much so He came and gave His life in place of our own. How can we not desire to worship this mighty God!

The Glory of the Lord Leaves the Temple

In Ezekiel, we find the apostasy of Israel is so pronounced; God decides to leave the temple Solomon had built.

Ezekiel 10:4, *"And the glory of the Lord went up from the cherub to the threshold of the house, and the house was filled with the cloud, and the court was filled with the brightness of the glory of the Lord."*

The cloud is an indication of divine presence which was first seen at the Red Sea. It guided the people in their wanderings in the wilderness (also shade [Ex. 13:21–22; Ps. 78:14; 105:39]). It appeared atop Mount Sinai (Ex. 24).

Ezekiel 10:18, *"Then the glory of the Lord went out from the threshold of the house and stood over the cherubim."*

The Return of the Glory of the Lord

The day will come when the glory of the Lord will once again appear. The first time Jesus came was as a babe, to be our Savior. The next time will be when He comes as the KING of kings in His glory. Matthew 25:31 says, *"When the Son of Man comes in his glory, and all the angels with him, then he will sit on his glorious throne."*

Our Christian lives are to make a difference, not only in our own lives, but also in the lives with whom we interact. So much so when Jesus does finally return, we will be ready to walk into the Holy City with Him to finally meet our heavenly Father.

While we may not see the cloud of glory today, we can experience the glory of God in our interactions with humankind. We can savor the glory of God as we examine, dwell within His Word. We can encounter the glory of God in His second book—nature.

Questions to Ponder:

How can I experience the beauty of being God's servant in the world today?

What will it take for me to acknowledge the glory of God whenever He demonstrates it in my life?

Take Away Notes:

Divine Consent, Divine Denial

Exodus 28: 29–30 (NIV), *"Whenever Aaron enters the Holy Place, he will bear the names of the sons of Israel over his heart on the breastpiece of decision as a continuing memorial before the Lord."*

"And in the breastpiece of judgment you shall put the Urim and the Thummim, and they shall be on Aaron's heart, when he goes in before the Lord. Thus, Aaron shall bear the judgment of the people of Israel on his heart before the Lord regularly" (ESV).

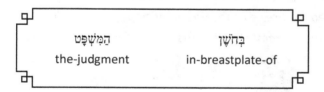

הַמִּשְׁפָּט   בַּחֹשֶׁן

the-judgment   in-breastplate-of

"At the right and left of the breastplate were two large stones of great brilliancy. These were known as the Urim and Thummim. By them, the will of God was made known through the high priest. When questions were brought for decision before the Lord, a halo of light encircling the precious stone at the right was a token of the divine consent or approval, while a cloud shadowing the stone at the left was an evidence of denial or disapprobation."[92]

---

[92] White, *Patriarchs and Prophets*, p. 351

Exodus 28:15, *"You shall make a breastpiece of judgment, in skilled work. In the style of the ephod you shall make it—of gold, blue and purple and scarlet yarns, and fine twined linen shall you make it."*

Skilled Work – The breastplate was a "cunning work." The word cunning, when used as an adjective in the context of the scriptures, means skillful or skillfully devised. This means it was crafted with careful deliberation and represents how God crafts His church with the same mindset. We are God's workmanship (Ephesians 2:10, *"For we are his workmanship, created in Christ Jesus for good works, which God prepared beforehand, that we should walk in them."*) and He has not haphazardly thrown us together but has recreated us in the image of his Son.

Gold – Demonstrates God's divinity. We will reveal our faith and love as we are tried in the fire. Our faith and love will be made pure as we go through the afflictions, difficulties, and trials in our lives (Revelation 3:18, *"I counsel you to buy from me gold refined by fire, so that you may be rich, and white garments so that you may clothe yourself and the shame of your nakedness may not be seen, and salve to anoint your eyes, so that you may see."* Verses 14:12, *"Here is a call for the endurance of the saints, those who keep the commandments of God and the faith of Jesus."* Malachi 3:3, *"He will sit as a refiner and purifier of silver, and he will purify the sons of Levi and refine them like gold and silver, and they will belong to the Lord, bringers of an offering in righteousness."*)

In my younger years, I tried to understand what the difference between test/trial and temptation was. My mother suggested, if I had something to learn it was a trial, and this came from God. If I was thinking only of my own desires, it was temptation, and this came from Satan.

Even with this definition, I still have problems today deciding whether a test/trial or temptation. So, we must remain alert, be aware of our circumstances, acknowledge the source as soon as possible. This will make the decision easier as we can learn the lesson or turn from the path of sin earlier rather than later.

> **Blue** – Represents the Ten Commandments—God's law. (Numbers 15:37–41, *"The LORD SAID TO MOSES, 'Speak to the people of Israel, and tell them to make tassels on the corners of their garments throughout their generations, and to put a cord of blue on the tassel of each corner. And it shall be a tassel for you to look at and remember all the commandments of the LORD, TO DO THEM, NOT TO FOLLOW AFTER YOUR OWN HEART AND YOUR OWN EYES, WHICH YOU ARE INCLINED TO WHORE AFTER. So you shall remember and do all my commandments and be holy to your God. I am the LORD YOUR GOD, WHO BROUGHT YOU OUT OF THE LAND OF EGYPT TO BE YOUR GOD: I AM THE LORD YOUR GOD.'"*) Some scholars have suggested the tablets were sapphire blue stone.

Citing Exodus 24:9–10, *"Then Moses and Aaron, Nadab, and Abihu, and seventy of the elders of Israel went up, and they saw the God of Israel. There was under his feet as it were a pavement of sapphire stone (lapis lazuli), like the very heaven for clearness."* It has also been suggested God took this stone from His own throne.

Did God take the first tables from His own throne? Did God use blue stone upon which he inscribed the Ten Commandments? While these questions might make for interesting conversation, there is nothing in Scripture to indicate such. Suffice it to say, the tassels on their garments were like tassels on the garments of the priests. Thus, these tassels would remind the Israelites they should follow God as a *"kingdom of priests and a holy nation"* (Ex.19:6–1; Pet. 2:9).

God wrote these commandments with His own finger on the first set of tablets. After the first set was broken, He also wrote upon the tablets, He had Moses make to bring up the mount. Obedience is so much easier than disobedience. More effort is required when disobedience occurs.

Three times we are told God wrote with His finger. The first time is here on the mount, writing the Ten Commandments on stone. (God commands obedience.) The second time, we see God writing on the wall in the hall of Belshazzar as he showed contempt for the sacred vessels of God. (Daniel 5—God declares judgment.) The third time God is found writing occurred when Jesus was being tested by the scribes and Pharisees over the issue of adultery. (John 8—God shows compassion and forgiveness.)

Purple – Denotes Jesus' royal status—His kingdom. (Judges 8:26, *"The weight of the golden earrings that he requested was 1,700 shekels of gold, besides the crescent ornaments and the pendants and the purple garments worn by the kings of Midian, and besides the collars that were around the necks of their camels."*) Gideon had just defeated the Midianites. Stripping of the purple robes denotes defeat and removal of their title of "king."

Purple dye was not easily accessible and therefore was meant mainly for the rulers. Acts 16:14 tells the story of Lydia, a seller of purple. This woman was staying in Philippi when she heard the gospel from Paul. *"One who heard us was a woman named Lydia, from the city of Thyatira, a seller of purple goods, who was a worshiper of God. The Lord opened her heart to pay attention to what was said by Paul."* She was later baptized along with her household, committing her life to the King of kings.

Scarlet – Symbolizes the service and sacrifice of Jesus. (Hebrews 9:22, *"Indeed, under the law almost everything is purified with blood, and without the shedding of blood there is no forgiveness* *of sins."*) Through Christ's death, His blood purifies us from our sin. His service in the heavenly sanctuary includes judgment on our behalf. Without His service and without His sacrifice, we could have no hope and thus no future (Jer. 29:11).

White/Fine Twined Linen—Refers to the purity of Jesus Himself—His righteousness, His truth. (First Peter 1:8–9, *"Though you have not seen him, you love him. Though you do not now see him, you believe in him and rejoice with joy that is inexpressible and filled with glory, obtaining the outcome of your faith, the salvation of your souls."*; Rev. 19:8 *"it was granted her to clothe herself with fine linen, bright and pure"*— for the fine linen is the righteous deeds of the saints."*) As we take on the character of Jesus, so He covers us with His righteousness, His purity.

Ezekiel 16:10, 13: *"I clothed you also with embroidered cloth and shod you with fine leather. I wrapped you in fine linen and covered you with silk.... Thus, you were adorned with gold and silver, and your clothing was of fine linen and silk and embroidered cloth."*

רִקְמָה Embroidered cloth - truths that are a matter of memory-knowledge

בַּשֵּׁשׁ cambric sheen - Fine Linen – purity of Jesus

מֶשִׁי gossamer - Silk – spiritual truths

Leviticus 8:8 (NIV), *"He placed the breastpiece on him and put the Urim and Thummim in the breastpiece."*

Urim and Thummim – Literally means "lights and perfections" (or curses). The Bible indicates that the Urim gave two types of answer.

"All sorts of fanciful explanations have been put forward, including that the items may have glowed, that they had secret words engraved on them, or that they were ancient artifacts with magical powers. However, it should be noted that 1 Samuel 14:41 [*'Therefore Saul said, O Lord God of Israel, why have you not answered your servant this day? If this guilt is in me or in Jonathan my son, O Lord, God of Israel, give Urim. But if this guilt is in your people Israel, give Thummim.'* And 1 Samuel 28:6, *'And when Saul inquired of the Lord, the Lord did not answer him, either by dreams, or by Urim, or by prophets.'*] makes clear a definite answer was not always obtainable, so it may not have been as simple as tossing two stones on ground. Moses never used them; they were given for the high priest in aiding those who could not find God's guidance any other way."[93]

In 1 Samuel 14, Saul had commanded his people to fast as they were pursuing and fighting their enemies. Jonathan, not knowing this, ate some honey which revived him in the battle. Saul foolishly sought the Lord's approval, which while it might appear God did, the people refused to kill Jonathan.

In 1 Samuel 28, Samuel was dead. Saul attempted to enquire of the Urim and Thummim, but God did not answer. Why? Because Saul had not walked with God for years, so he turned to the witch at Endor for guidance.

For Moses' replacement, God selected Joshua, who then was to stand before Eleazar, the high priest, to seek God's direction (Num. 27:18–21).

While we do not really understand everything about the Urim and Thummim, we do know God used these to guide the ancient Israelites up to about the time of David.

---

[93] "How did the Urim and the Thummim function?" Bible.org, January 1, 2001, accessed February 9, 2020, https://bible.org/question/how-did-urim-and-thummim-function.

The Urim and Thummim were used at critical moments in the history of God's people when special divine guidance was needed. The civil leader was expected to make use of this means for all important matters for which he needed direction. Although referred to in Ezra 2:63 and Nehemiah 7:65, there is no convincing evidence that the Urim and Thummim were used after the time of David.

Doing What Was Right in His Own Eyes

In the book of Judges, we find two references, 17:6 and 21:25, *"In those days there was no king in Israel. Everyone did what was right in his own eyes."*

Did Israel not have a king? Of course, God was their king. Unfortunately, by this time, the Israelites did not recognize God as their king. They were more interested in being like the nations which surrounded them; the nations they were to destroy from off the face of the earth—the Canaanites, the Hittites, the Amorites, the Perizzites, the Hivites, and the Jebusites.

> **The Canaanites** – "They were a wicked, idolatrous people descended from Noah's grandson, Canaan, who was a son of Ham (Gen. 9:18).... Canaanites is used more broadly to refer to all the inhabitants of the land, including the Hivites, Girgashites, Jebusites, Amorites, Hittites, and Perizzites.... Despite a long campaign against the inhabitants of Canaan, there remained several pockets of Canaanites in Israel after the land had been divided among the twelve tribes.... The partial obedience of Israel, resulting in these Canaanite citadels, caused much trouble throughout the time of the Judges.[94]

---

[94] "Who were the Canaanites?" Got Questions, accessed February 9, 2020, https://www.gotquestions.org/Canaanites.html.

Proverbs 14:12, *"There is a way that seems right to a man, but its end is the way of death."*

"In deciding upon any course of action we are not to ask whether we can see that harm will result from it, but, whether it is in keeping with the will of God."[95]

Proverbs 16:25, *"There is a way that seems right to a man, but its end is the way of death."*

"Ignorance is no excuse for error or sin, when there is every opportunity to know the will of God. A man is traveling and comes to a place where there are several roads and a guide board indicating where each one leads. If he disregards the guide board, and takes whichever road seems to him to be right, he may be ever so sincere, but will in all probability find himself on the wrong road."[96]

Deuteronomy 12:7–9 7, *"There, in the presence of the Lord your God, you and your households shall eat and rejoice in all you do, because the Lord your God has blessed you. You are not to do as we are doing here today, where everyone does what seems right in his own eyes. For you have not yet come to the resting place and the inheritance the Lord your God is giving you."*

At this time, the Israelites were sacrificing as they traveled from place to place. But in the future, Moses was telling them they would only sacrifice in a designated place. Since the tabernacle had not yet found a resting place, they were free to worship in various geographical

---

[95] White, *Patriarchs and Prophets*, p. 634

[96] White, *The Great Controversy Between Christ and Satan*, p. 598

locations, but it was always near the location where the tabernacle had been erected.

Leviticus 17 spells out the criteria to be used in relation to butchering clean animals for eating, which could also be used for sacrifices. Since the Israelites tended to worship other deities, God set the standard.

Curiously, the practice of posing "yes" and "no" questions to the gods of the heathen is a well-known practice—Babylonian and Assyrian are two such examples. So why would God allow the Israelites to follow this same practice? Do we not ask for signs from God today? Maybe we should start trusting God and knowing Him better day by day through Bible study, prayer, and communion with God, so we won't have to be asking Him for signs. As we learn to trust Him more, we will find ourselves putting our will into His will. Continuously, we are to pray. (First Thessalonians 5:17—an attitude of God-consciousness and God-surrender that we carry with us all the time.)

Questions to Ponder:

Am I trusting God enough not to ask His guidance?

Why am I NOT asking?

Am I trusting myself more than trusting in God's guidance?

Take Away Notes:

Divine Testimony—Spoken By God

Exodus 31:18; 32:16, *"And he gave to Moses, when he had finished **speaking** with him on Mount Sinai, the two tablets of the
testimony, tablets of stone, written with the finger of God.... The
tablets were **the work of God**; the writing was the writing of
God, engraved on the tablets."* (Emphasis mine.)

Testimony – "A formal written or spoken statement, especially
one given in a court of law."[97]

W hen God presented the covenant agreement, He was presenting
His side of the covenant proposal.

"Three months after leaving Egypt the Children of Israel have
arrived at the base of the Sinai Mountain. Moses, acting the
part of Mediator, meets first with God and then relates to the
people the conditions for this upcoming covenant. Exodus 19:5–
6, *'Now therefore, **if you will indeed obey my voice and keep
my covenant**, you shall be my treasured possession among all*

---

[97] "Testimony" definition, Lexico, accessed February 9, 2020, https://
en.oxforddictionaries.com/definition/testimony.

*peoples, **for all the earth is mine**; 6 and you shall be to me a kingdom of priests and a holy nation.'"* God declares His exclusive claim—all the earth belongs to Him, including the people. He can decide what, when, where, why, and how He will deal with His creation. He has declared He sovereign authority over His creation. Here, on this Mountain, He has declared who His people will be. Wisely, He has also given these people His ultimatum, He has made one stipulation – they are to 'obey His voice and keep His covenant." (Emphasis mine.)

Today, "the church is the people of God, the people who belong to God, who claim God as their Father and Saviour, and who have been redeemed by Christ and who **obey Him**."[98] (Emphasis mine.)

Included in this covenant agreement was the response of the Israelites as recorded in Exodus 19:8, *"All the people answered together and said, **'All that the Lord has spoken we will do.'** And Moses reported the words of the people to the Lord."* This is the first of three times the children of Israel will make this statement, this promise, this vow.

These people have recently witnessed the power of God in their behalf. They watched the ten plagues against the Egyptians, even experienced the first three plagues. They observed the destruction of Egypt, participated in the crossing of the Red Sea, were fed by the manna from heaven. They have traveled and camped for the past three months and now, these people are encamped around the base of the Sinai mountain. Moses has returned from his first trip up this mountain to meet with this God who has brought them here. Here, where Moses first met God in the burning bush who had told him already who He is. (Exodus 3:12, *"He said, 'But I will be with you, and this shall be the sign for you, that I have sent you: when you have brought the people out of Egypt, you shall serve God on this mountain.'"*)

---

[98] "Oneness in Christ," *Adult Sabbath School Bible Study Guide*, October–December 2018, p. 47

SPOKEN WORD

Exodus 20:1, *"And **God spoke** all these words saying,"* God introduces the Testimony, the Ten Commandments, Ten Words, by reminding them He was the One who brought them not only out of Egypt, but also, out of bondage, out of the house of slavery (Deut. 5:15).

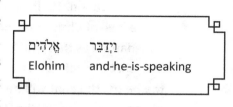

אֱלֹהִים   וַיְדַבֵּר
Elohim   and-he-is-speaking

"I AM the LORD." He identifies Himself as the Deliverer. Obedience to the Commandments is based upon the experience of God's grace. Both Old and New Testaments emphasizes God's

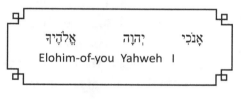

אֱלֹהֶיךָ   יְהוָה   אָנֹכִי
Elohim-of-you Yahweh I

grace as the foundation, the heart, the source for obedience (Ephesians 2:8–10, *"For by grace you have been saved through faith. And this is not your own doing; it is the gift of God, not a result of works, so that no one may boast. For we are his workmanship, created in Christ Jesus for good works, which God prepared beforehand, that we should walk in them."*)

Grace costs absolutely nothing, neither can grace be earned. Only through the transformation of God within our hearts and minds can we experience this grace. As we understand and become more involved in God's working in our lives, as we embrace a relationship with God, we can be transformed to live a life of works for God. But we must ever remember the works we do are not for our earnings. But with gratitude, with thankfulness in heart and mind, acknowledging God gives His grace to unworthy, undeserving, despicable sinners as we are, turning us into valuable, treasured, beloved human beings fit for His kingdom.

"There are those who profess to serve God while they rely upon their own efforts to obey His law, to form a right character, and secure salvation. Their hearts are not moved by any deep sense of the love of Christ, but they seek to perform the duties of the Christian life as that which God requires of them in order to gain heaven. Such religion is worth nothing. **When Christ dwells in the heart, the soul will be so filled with His love, with the joy of communion with Him, that it will cleave to Him; and in the contemplation of Him, self will be forgotten.** Love to Christ will be the spring of action. Those who feel the constraining love of God do not ask how little may be given to meet the requirements of God; they do not ask for the lowest standard, but aim at perfect conformity to the will of their Redeemer. With earnest desire, they yield all and manifest an interest proportionate to the value of the object which they seek. A profession of Christ without this deep love is mere talk, dry formality, and heavy drudgery."[99] (Emphasis mine.)

"It is not the length of time we labor but our willingness and fidelity in the work that makes it acceptable to God. In all our service a full surrender of self is demanded. The smallest duty done in sincerity and self-forgetfulness is more pleasing to God than the greatest work when marred with self-seeking. He looks to see how much of the spirit of Christ we cherish, and how much of the likeness of Christ our work reveals. **He regards more the love and faithfulness with which we work than the amount we do.**"[100] (Emphasis mine.)

God spoke the Commandments from the top of Mount Sinai initially. When the children of Israel heard His voice, they were afraid, they were

---

[99] Ellen G. White, *Steps to Christ*, (Nampa, ID: Pacific Press Publishing Association, 1997) p. 44.

[100] White, *Christ's Object Lessons*, p. 402

terrified, their anxiety level reached new heights. They told Moses to have God speak to him and then he could speak God's words to them. Exodus 20:18–19, *"Now when all the people saw the thunder and the flashes of lightning and the sound*

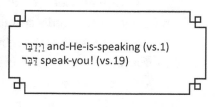

וַיְדַבֵּר and-He-is-speaking (vs.1)
דַּבֵּר speak-you! (vs.19)

of the trumpet and the mountain smoking, the people were afraid and trembled, and they stood far off and said to Moses, 'You speak to us, and we will listen; but do not let God speak to us, lest we die.'"

We assume God bellowed His conditions for the covenant, His voice thundered from the mount, He shouted to be heard by the multitude. Have we misinterpreted the voice of God?

First Kings 19:9–13 tells an interesting story of Elijah's encounter with God. A strong wind, an earthquake, a fire, yet God was NOT there. A low whisper is the voice of God heard by Elijah. Sometimes, though, God does have to raise His voice for us to hear Him speak to us.

דַּקָּה   דְּמָמָה
gentle   stillness

Verse 12, "and after the earthquake, a fire, but the Lord was not in the fire. And after the fire the sound of a low whisper."

Then there came a still, small voice, and the prophet covered his head before the presence of the Lord. His petulance was silenced, his spirit softened and subdued. He now knew that a quiet trust, a firm reliance on God, would ever find for him a present help in time of need.

"It is not always the most learned presentation of God's truth that convicts and converts the soul. Not by eloquence or logic are men's hearts reached, but by the sweet influences of the Holy Spirit, which operate quietly yet surely in transforming and developing character. It is the still, small voice of the Spirit of God that has power to change the heart."[101]

---

[101] White, *Prophets and Kings*, p. 168

There have been times when I preach, someone comes and tells me they appreciated a certain point I made in that sermon. I sometimes would not recall that thought and would recognize the Holy Spirit spoke to that individual's heart causing them to hear something I might not have remembered even saying. I have also had to pause as I realized God was saying something to me. Sometimes I was directed to share and sometimes I knew this was for my ears alone. God does not have to raise His voice to be heard by a heart that is tuned to His voice.

There will be a time though when the voice of God will cry out, will shout. In 1 Thessalonians 4:16, *"For the Lord himself will descend from heaven with a **cry of command**, with the voice of an archangel, and with the sound of the trumpet of God. And the dead in Christ will rise first."* (Emphasis mine.) To awaken the dead, Christ will give a cry of command or shout (KJV; NASB) or loud command (NIV). There will be no soft-spoken word spoken at this event.

Moses Upon the Mountain

Moses was the mediator between God and the people. After God pronounced the Ten Words, Moses was called up to the mountain to meet with God. In chapters 21–23, we find God dictating to Moses various laws about slaves and servants, animal control, social justice, Sabbaths and festivals.

In chapter 24, Moses brings these laws, which he had written, to the people. Verse 3 says, *"Moses came and told the people all the words of the Lord and all the rules. And all the people answered with one voice and said, '**All the words that the Lord has spoken we will do.**'"* (Emphasis mine.)

Finally, the third time, the children of Israel declare in Exodus 24:7, *"Then he took the Book of the Covenant and read it in the hearing of the people. And they said, '**All that the Lord has spoken we will do, and we will be obedient.**'"* (Emphasis mine.) The people have declared, they have made their choice, and they have stated they were willing to do and to be obedient.

Three times we see recorded the people have declared, *"All the words that the Lord has spoken we will do"* (Ex. 19:8; 24:3, 7). It is easy enough to say something, but quite different when we put our words into action. At this end of the story, it is again easy for us to condemn the children of Israel in turning their backs to God. Regrettably, we have not changed our ways either. All we can do is lean fully and completely upon the God of our salvation, seeking His grace and His mercy. He will not fail to support us.

Sacrifice of Covenant

Sacrifice was made. Moses took half of the blood and sprinkled it on the altar. The other half, he sprinkled upon the people.

The blood of a sacrifice always belongs to God. In Leviticus, blood is sprinkled to cleanse from sin. Here blood sprinkling is used to bind the people to God. Jesus, in Matthew 26:28, uses the cup to symbolize His blood and combines these two ceremonies.[102]

Matthew 26:28, *"for this is my blood of the covenant, which is poured out for many for the forgiveness of sins."* While some translations insert "New Covenant," Jesus has declared His blood will be used instead of the old sacrificial system given to the children of Israel on Mount Sinai. Today, we consider the New Covenant to have done away with the Ten Words, the Ten Commandments. But what has been replaced, there is no more animal sacrifice to be considered. Jesus' atoning blood covers our sins.

The Review

In reviewing the history of the children of Israel's experiences, travels, and exploits, Moses shares with the new generation what happened when God first spoke to their parents. This generation had not

---

[102] Andrews Study Bible Commentary, Exodus 24:8

experienced the presence of God on the mount, nor the construction of the wilderness tabernacle, nor were they present at the time of the golden calf episode (Ex. 32).

> Deuteronomy 5:22–27, *"These words the Lord **spoke** to all your assembly at the mountain out of the midst of the fire, the cloud, and the thick darkness, with a loud voice; and he added no more. And he **wrote** them on two tablets of stone and gave them to me. And as soon as you heard the voice out of the midst of the darkness, while the mountain was burning with fire, you came near to me, all the heads of your tribes, and your elders. And you said, 'Behold, the Lord our God has shown us his glory and greatness, and we have heard his voice out of the midst of the fire. This day we have seen God speak with man, and man still live. Now therefore why should we die? For this great fire will consume us. If we hear the voice of the Lord our God any more, we shall die. For who is there of all flesh, that has heard the voice of the living God speaking out of the midst of fire as we have, and has still lived? Go near and hear all that the Lord our God will say and speak to us all that the Lord our God will speak to you, and **we will hear and do it.**"* (Emphasis mine.)

As each new generation rises, each must hear the covenant, understand the requirements, then make the choice of obedience or death. It is that simple. Obey and live or disobey and die. This has been God's provision, God's prerequisite, God's condition to each of His creation people. Choice, election, decision. This has and always will be a privilege God has given to every one of us. This privilege is NOT a right. From the beginning God has given us this freedom, this favor. We must be careful not to assume our choice as a right. God did not have to give us choice, but He did. We have the responsibility to look into this matter of God being our Creator, our Redeemer, and with a mind (which He has also given us) that looks at all the aspects of this Creator, created relationship, thus we make an informed choice. God will respect our choice. We must then accept our choice will have consequences.

Consequences—whether evil or good, death or life, pain and sorrow, or peace and grace. Every choice has a consequence, a result, an outcome.

Our parents, Adam and Eve, were given this opportunity. They chose to believe the, lie and today, we live out the consequences not only of their disobedience, but also our continued disobedience.

Questions to Ponder:

Am I willing to enter into a covenant with God, my Creator, my Redeemer?

Do I consider my choice(s) of importance?

What choice am I making today?

Take Away Notes:

DIVINE TESTIMONY—
WRITTEN WORD

Exodus 31:18; 32:16: *"And he gave to Moses, when he had fin-ished speaking with him on Mount Sinai, the two tablets of the testimony, tablets of stone, written with the finger of God…. The* **tablets were the work of God***; the* **writing was the writing of God***, engraved on the tablets."* (Emphasis mine.)

The Tablets

The tablets were the work of God, not angels or men. The stones were created and shaped by God. "The let-ters in which the law was written were of His framing, devising, and engraving; and this was to show that this law was his own, and contained his mind and will; and to give the greater dignity and authority to it, and to deter men from breaking it." [103]

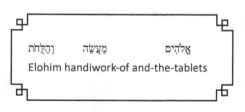

Imagine, for a moment, Moses' response when He was handed the tablets upon which God had written His Ten Words, His ten conditions

---

[103] "Exodus 3:16," Bible Study Tools, accessed February 9, 2020, https://www.biblestudytools.com/commentaries/gills-exposition-of-the-bible/exodus-32-16.html.

for this covenant. Here is a man who is eighty plus years old. He is at the upper echelon of the mount. He will be carrying these tablets down the mountain to give these terms of reference to the people. We often picture these tablets as being quite large and thus quite heavy. What a burden for Moses to carry.

We purchase a house, so we sign a document that we will follow the terms of the mortgage. It does not matter whether we think the terms are too harsh, we signed an agreement

> Matthew 11:29–30 says, *"Take my yoke upon you, and learn from me, for I am gentle and lowly in heart, and you will find rest for your souls. For my yoke is easy, and my burden is light."*

For many generations, men have placed upon the ears of the people that the law is burdensome; God's ways are too difficult to handle. So much so that God decided to do away with His law and so hung His law upon the cross. This could not be further from the truth—God's truth. God does not change (Mal. 3:6; Heb. 13:8). We, on the other hand, do change. We are unstable because we change. God calls us to be steadfast, constant, faithful, and yes, even as God is. As we focus upon God, we become resolved to become more like our Creator.

The Apostasy – Golden Calf

The story of the golden calf is placed between these two verses. How quickly the children of Israel were to abandon their initial resolve, ***"All that the Lord has spoken we will do, and we will be obedient"*** (Ex. 24:7). Three times they made this proclamation, and within days of this declaration, they abandoned their resolve and turned back in mind and spirit to where they originally had been—in Egypt. Worshiping the Egyptian gods, they determined to build a replica of a god they remembered.

We are no different today. Our old habits tend to show up at the most inappropriate times and cause us to fall into temptation so easily. Paul, in Romans 7:15–17, *"For I do not understand my own actions. For I do not do what I want, but I do the very thing I hate. Now if I do what I do not want, I agree with the law, that it is good. So now it is no longer I who do it, but sin that dwells within me."* Paul recognizes there is a conflict of two different natures. While we want to take on the character of Jesus, we find our selfish nature interposing, interrupting, and interfering in our efforts to be more like Christ.

Thus, Paul declares in verses 24–25, *"Wretched man that I am! Who will deliver me from this body of death?* **Thanks be to God through Jesus Christ our Lord!** *So then, I myself serve the law of God with my mind, but with my flesh I serve the law of sin."* (Emphasis mine.) Only with the help of the Holy Spirit, through Jesus and God the Father, are we able to embrace God's character and accept the righteousness of Jesus to infill us with power to overcome the selfish man each of us has inbred.

The Tablets in the Ark of the Covenant

The inclusion of the information about the two tablets of the Testimony is linked to the fact that the law was to be deposited in the Ark of the Covenant in the most holy place (Exodus 25:16, *"And you shall put into the ark the Testimony which I will give you."*) It also links the prescriptive tabernacle construction section with the golden calf story, where the tablets play a major role. [104]

God Tests Moses

God knew what they were doing and told Moses. In His anger, God was ready to destroy Israel. Moses pleaded with Him.

"As Moses interceded for Israel, his timidity was lost in his deep interest and love for those for whom he had, in the hands of

---

[104] Andrews Study Bible, Exodus 31:18 comments

God, been the means of doing so much. The Lord listened to his pleadings and granted his unselfish prayer. **God had proved His servant; He had tested his faithfulness** and **his love** for that erring, ungrateful people, and nobly had **Moses endured the trial**. His interest in Israel sprang from no selfish motive."[105] (Emphasis mine.)

Moses could have failed, but he put self aside in the interest of His God and God's people. God did not need to be reminded. He remembers even today our frailties, our failures, and our disappointments. God also remembers our position as His children and accepts us as we are, provided we remain obedient to the covenant. Revelation 14:12 (KJV), *"Here is the patience of the saints: here are they who keep the Commandments of God and the faith of Jesus."* From beginning to end, the condition of the covenant is obedience. We either obey God or Satan, it is that simple.

The Written Tablets

Why would God need to write the Commandments on the tablets in the first place?

In the beginning, Adam and Eve had hearts of flesh and God had been able to write His law upon their hearts. Once sin entered, the hearts of His people began to be turned into stone. By the time of Israel's departure from Egypt, the children of Israel were "stiff-necked" and stubborn. God had to write on tablets of stones because their hearts were stone. Ezekiel 26:35 tells us, *"And I will give you a new heart, and a new spirit I will put within you. And I will remove the heart of stone from your flesh and give you a heart of flesh."*

The Israelites were so immersed in the worship of pagan (Egyptian) gods, they would not have been able to remember and obey the precepts of God unless it was written down. Their character had been so

---

[105] White, *Patriarchs and Prophets*, p. 319

corrupted from the years of absorbing the foreign elements, they would need to have the written Word to help them remember. Today, we also need the written Word of God to help us remember who God is and what He is planning for us.

> Jeremiah 31:33, *"For this is the covenant that I will make with the house of Israel after those days, declares the Lord: I will put my law within them, and I will write it on their hearts. And I will be their God, and they shall be my people."*

Hebrews 8:10 quotes from Jeremiah 31:33. We are sinners in need of a Savior. Only God can turn our hearts from stone and make them flesh. Only God can provide us the strength to go from day to day in His power. Only God can take our stubbornness and hard-heartedness and make us into His children filled with His character, His essence, His personality, His influence.

The terms of the "Old Covenant" were to obey and live. *"If a man do, he shall even live in them"* (Ezk. 20:11; Lev. 18:5); but *"cursed be he that confirmeth not all the words of this law to do them"* (Deut. 27:26). The "New Covenant" was established upon "better promises"—the promise of forgiveness of sins and of the grace of God to renew the heart and bring it into harmony with the principles of God's law.[106]

Again, we understand the covenant formula. This covenant was always to have been written upon the hearts of God's people. Through the aid of the Holy Spirit, this can be accomplished, provided obedience and commitment is present.

Deuteronomy 30:5–6 tells us, *"the Lord your God will bring you into the land that your fathers possessed, that you may possess it. And he will make you more prosperous and numerous than your fathers. And the Lord your God will circumcise your heart and the heart of your offspring, so that you will love the Lord your God with all your heart and*

---

[106] White, *Patriarchs and Prophets*, p. 382

with all your soul, that you may live." Thus, bringing to fruition the great commandment God gave them in chapter 6:4.

> Micah 6:6–8, *"'With what shall I come before the Lord, and bow myself before God on high?*
>
> *Shall I come before him with burnt offerings, with calves a year old?*
>
> *Will the Lord be pleased with thousands of rams, with ten thousands of rivers of oil?*
>
> *Shall I give my firstborn for my transgression, the fruit of my body for the sin of my soul?'*
>
> *He has told you, O man, what is good; and what does the Lord require of you but **to do justice**, and **to love kindness**, and **to walk humbly with your God**?"* (Emphasis mine.)

> "From age to age, these counsels were repeated by the servants of Jehovah to those who were in danger of falling into habits of formalism and of forgetting to show mercy."[107]

Moses' Reaction

Moses went down and saw what the Israelites were doing—they had abandoned the precepts completely and indulged in gluttony, feasting, worshiping of a golden calf. Moses threw down the tablets God had previously written upon.

---

[107] White, *Prophets and Kings*, p. 326

Why? Because the Israelites had broken the covenant which they had promised back in Exodus 19:8, *"All that the Lord commands we will do."* Obedience is the response God expects from His covenant people. Moses throwing the tablets down, the children of Israel seeing the tablets broken into pieces, was a public and ritual demonstration that the covenant has been broken.

After the first tablets were broken by Moses, God instructs him to cut out two more tablets, bring them up the mountain and He would write the testimony again. Exodus 34:1, *"The Lord said to Moses, 'Cut for yourself two tablets of stone like the first, and I will write on the tablets the words that were of the first tablets, which you broke.'"*

A question needs to be asked, why would God have Moses cut out the stone and carry the stone up the mountain for God to rewrite the Commandments?

Various scenarios can be considered as to why Moses have to make the tablets the second time:

1) Moses, who previously talked God out of consuming the nation of Israel in His wrath, came down and saw firsthand what had made God so angry. "The anger of Moses grew hot and he broke the tables of stone. The act was based on the same anger that might have consumed the nation of Israel had not Moses interceded. It was, in essence, the same thought of God. God's thought was, these people cannot be My people any longer. They are sinful, they disobey Me, they cannot continue with Me because I am a holy God.... Why would they need the tables of stone any longer since the covenant was broken and there was no longer a covenant relationship between the nation of Israel and the God of Israel?"[108]

---

[108] The Orange Mailman, "Why did Moses break the stone tablets?" The Orange Mailman, May 30, 2013, accessed February 9, 2020, https://theorangemailmanmyblog. wordpress.com/2013/05/30/why-did-moses-break-the-stone-tablets/.

God, in His mercy, reached out to the children of Israel, forgave their grievous sins, thus demonstrating His amazing grace. He encouraged them to go forward in a renewal of the covenant with Him. God worked with His people in their sinful estate, in reestablishing the covenant which they had broken. All this is God's doing, not theirs, not ours today.

2) Because Moses made the tablets according to God's command, it demonstrates God's willingness to place Moses in His own position. The children of Israel wanted Moses to intervene for them with God. So, when they were apostatizing, God gave them leave to have Moses as their "god" rather than God Himself.

Moses, being such a humble man, did not take on this position. He remained loyal to God throughout his term as leader of the Israelites. Only when he placed himself as an equal to God, did Moses demonstrate his fallibility as a man. This occurred when God had told Moses to speak to the rock for water, but Moses struck the rock, and in Numbers 20:10, *"Then Moses and Aaron gathered the assembly together before the rock, and he said to them, 'Hear now, you rebels: **shall we** bring water for you out of this rock?'"* For this, God prohibited Moses from entering Canaan to prevent validation of his claim of God-ship to the children of Israel.

3) The Bible goes way out of its way to EXPLICITLY say that God cut the stones for the first tablets out of the mountain (Ex. 32:16), and then just as explicitly says that Moses made the second tablets (Ex. 34:1).

There is one other place where God "cuts" out stone without hands. In the second chapter of Daniel, the pagan king, Nebuchadnezzar, had a dream. In this dream he sees a stone cut from a mountain without hands. Daniel 2:45, *"just as you saw that a stone was cut from a mountain by no human hand, and that it broke in pieces the iron, the bronze, the clay, the silver, and the gold. A great God has made known to the king what shall be after this. The dream is certain, and its interpretation sure."*

Defiled Tablets

Moses, in making the tablets, would have "defiled" the stone according to God's earlier command about building altars. Exodus 20:25 say; *"If you make me an altar of stone, you shall not build it of hewn stones, for if you wield your tool on it you profane it."* Moses would have had to use hammer and chisel for making these tablets.

Why use "defiled" stone when the stone God used was holy?

Ezekiel 36:26, *"And I will give you a new heart, and a new spirit I will put within you. And I will remove the heart of stone from your flesh and give you a heart of flesh."* When our hearts become hardened to the Spirit's touch, our hearts take on the quality of stone. God wants to remove the stoniness of our hearts, so He can write upon our hearts His words of love.

Psalm 51:10, *"Create in me a clean heart, O God, and renew a right [steadfast] spirit within me."*

Jesus, the Stone

Various scripture is used to determine the stone to represent Jesus (1 Cor. 10:4; Ps. 18:2). Thus, we use the stone for the Ten Commandments to represent Jesus and go one step further and acknowledge the Commandments themselves are characteristics of Jesus.

1) Exodus 19:5–6, *"Now therefore, if you will indeed obey my voice and keep my covenant, you shall be my treasured possession among all peoples, for all the earth is mine; and you shall be to me a kingdom of priests and a holy nation."* This is what God wanted in the first place. When He presented Moses with the

213

Commandments written on the first tablet, God was presenting Himself to the people. But Moses broke these because of the sins of the people during the golden calf episode.

Today, we consider the giving of the tablets as the Old Covenant, but is this really the truth? By breaking the tablets, the "Old Covenant" was broken. Thus "Old Covenant" was never accepted in the first place!

First Peter 2:7–9, *"So the honor is for you who believe, but for those who do not believe "The stone that the builders rejected has become the cornerstone, But you are a chosen race, a royal priesthood, a holy nation, a people for his own possession, that you may proclaim the excellencies of him who called you out of darkness into his marvelous light."*

"This scripture is SPECIFICALLY, and ONLY talking about those who are called out of darkness; those who BELIEVE that Rock, Jesus; those who have the light of God's truth; those who are a ROYAL PRIESTHOOD and a HOLY nation, something Israel NEVER WAS! This is a NEW Covenant promise! And so was the promise in Exodus 19:5–6!"[109]

We must remember, God spoke these words to the Israelites, they were terrified, and asked for an intermediary. God wanted a personal relationship with the children of Israel. They rejected this. They wanted Moses over Jesus!

"The New Covenant is a covenant where God speaks to you directly, through His spirit; He influences you, guides you, looks

---

[109] "Moses: The First Commandment Breaker," The Simple Answers, May 10, 2010, accessed February 9, 2020, https://www.thesimpleanswers.com/2010/05/10/moses-the-first-commandment-breaker/.

on your heart and sees whether it's good or bad and judges you accordingly. There is no intermediary...it's you and [God]."[110]

As we consider this concept, we need to come to the conclusion, there has never been an Old Covenant and a New Covenant. This is something God has always wanted and still desires. He wants this personal relationship with each of His children!

Reconciling Us to God

Despite the apostasy of the children of Israel, God is still desiring and willing to renew the covenant. Throughout their history, through the ensuing centuries and up to today, God has been working to reconcile us to Himself. Second Corinthians 5:18–20, *"All this is from God, who through Christ reconciled us to himself and gave us the ministry of reconciliation; that is, in Christ God was reconciling the world to himself, not counting their trespasses against them, and entrusting to us the message of reconciliation. Therefore, we are ambassadors for Christ, God making his appeal through us. We implore you on behalf of Christ, be reconciled to God."*

Reconciling the World to Himself – καταλλαγὴν

"'Reconcile'—that is to reunite those who were originally united, but afterwards separated by the sin of man. This brings out the profound idea, which so especially characterizes these Epistles, of a

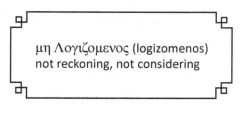

μη Λογιζομενος (logizomenos)
not reckoning, not considering

primeval unity of all created being in Christ, marred and broken by sin, and restored by His manifestation in human flesh."[111]

---

110   Ibid.

111   "Ephesians 2:16, Elliott's Commentary for English Readers," Bible Hub, accessed

First John 1:9, *"If we confess our sins, he is faithful and just to forgive us our sins and to cleanse us from all unrighteousness."*

"IF we confess"—means, if we acknowledge the blame, recognize the sin is our fault, not the fault of someone or something else.

Forgives and Cleans

God then forgives the sin and will clean the sin from our lives. Jeremiah 2:22, *"'Although you wash yourself with soap and use an abundance of cleansing powder, the stain of your guilt is still before me,' declares the Sovereign Lord."* We cannot do what God can do. We must submit to His cleansing. "The fuller was usually the dyer, since, before the woven cloth could be properly dyed, it must be freed from the oily and gummy substances naturally found on the raw fiber."[112]

Malachi 3:2, *"But who can endure the day of his coming? Who can stand when he appears? For he will be like a refiner's fire or a launderer's soap."* Though we often use this passage to indicate Jesus' Second Coming, this can also indicate the forgiveness of our sins. Who can stand before God while confessing our sin? Standing gives the connotation of equality and similar status with God. No one can do this. Only Jesus, the God-Man, can and is able to stand in His place.

The word translated "reconciliation" is it should be noted, the same as that rendered "atonement" in Romans 5:11 (KJV) *"And not only so,*

February 9, 2020, https://biblehub.com/commentaries/ephesians/2–16.htm.

[112] "Fuller," Bible Study Tools, accessed February 9, 2020, https://www.biblestudytools.com/dictionary/fuller/.

Many different substances were in ancient times used for cleansing. Among them were white clay, putrid urine, and the ashes of certain desert plants (Arabic *qali*, Biblical "soap"; Malachi 3:2). The fuller's shop was usually outside the city (2 Kin. 18:17; Isa. 7:3; 36:2), first, that he might have sufficient room to spread out his cloth for drying and sunning; and second, because of the offensive odors sometimes produced by his processes.

but we also joy in God through our Lord Jesus Christ, by whom we have now received the atonement."[113]

Not Counting Their Trespasses

Psalm 32:2, *"Blessed is the man against whom the Lord counts no iniquity, and in whose spirit, there is no deceit."*

God no longer charges our sins against us. We ask forgiveness, He freely forgives. There are no conditions set upon us for those sins of which we have been forgiven. God no more considers our forgiven sins of any consequence.

Entrusting to Us the Message of Reconciliation

While God is embracing the whole world to be reconciled to Himself, as Paul suggests in this segment, "entrusting us" is limited to those who embrace the reconciliation of God and then shares with others this gift of reconciliation. One step further then suggests the one who accepts the message of the "ambassador" accepts not only the messenger but also the sender in this situation with Jesus. And if accepting Jesus is accepting God the Father, and thus enjoy the reconciliation which the Father initiated in the first place.

Two Stories

Mark 9:27, *"But Jesus took him by the hand and lifted him up, and he arose."* Jesus had recently communed with Moses and Elijah on the Mount of Transfiguration. The three disciples with Jesus were Peter, James, and John. As they were coming down, they encountered the rest of the disciples trying to cast out the demon from a young boy.

Unfortunately, they were unsuccessful. Why? Jesus Himself

---

[113] "2 Corinthians 5:18, Elliot's Commentary for English Readers," accessed February 9, 2020, https://biblehub.com/commentaries/2_corinthians/5-18.htm.

explained in verse 29, *"And he said to them, 'This kind cannot be driven out by anything but prayer.'"* Some translations also add "fasting." The process of reconciliation demands prayer be a part of the process. We must remember who initiates reconciliation—God. So, we must ask Him to bring us back to Himself.

"What kind of prayer will drive out this type of demon? Some prayer lives lack consistency.... Others of us need sincerity.... Still others lack, well honesty."[114] The prayer of the father was one of desperation; sharing the pain from the depths of his being, he asked Jesus, the Creator, the Redeemer of the world: *"But if you can do anything, have compassion on us and help us"* (Mk. 9:22b). Initially, one might suggest the father has no faith, but he did have faith, he just needed a little more, for which He also asked Jesus.

To be reconciled to God demands continuous prayer, intimate conversations, a heart-to-heart discussion with our Father in heaven. Being willing to open our hearts and our minds to His guiding, His probing, His cleaning, His equipping, so we can be ready to be ambassadors for reconciliation.

We are the ones who leave our position, our responsibilities, our life path that God has ordained for us. God will either come Himself or send someone to seek us out and encourage our return.

John 13:20, *"Truly, truly, I say to you, whoever receives the one I send receives me, and whoever receives me receives the one who sent me."*

Second Story

Jesus was with His disciples at the last supper. He washed their feet and demonstrated what they were to do—to be ambassadors for Him. He told them, that as His messengers, if they were accepted by those who heard them, He also would accept them.

---

[114] Max Lucado, *He Still Moves Stones*, (Dallas, TX: Word Publishing, 1996), p. 97, 98.

It is not easy to be an ambassador for Jesus. Often, we are rejected, but we must remember, He was spurned as well. He knows what it feels like to be cast aside, to be scorned, to be discarded, to be abandoned, to be left alone.

He also has reassured us He would claim as His own those who accept our word. He would declare those who claim Him as their Savior, because of our words, part of His family. Thus, we all become children of the King of kings and Lord of lords.

This is the decision we must make consciously, mindfully, willfully, determinedly to make Jesus our Lord and Savior of our lives. Then, we are to take on the position of ambassador to seek out those who need Jesus in their lives, to share with them the good news as we know it. We are not talking doctrine, but relationship with our Creator. We can only testify to something of which we have intimate knowledge. There is no room for second-hand information.

First John 3:1, *"See what kind of love the Father has given to us, that we should be called children of God; and so, we are. The reason why the world does not know us is that it did not know him."*

We acknowledge God is LOVE. He fills us with His amazing love, we share this love with others, He refills us so we can continue to distribute. As we consider 1 Corinthians 13, we could easily insert GOD for LOVE. "If I speak in the tongues of men and of angels, but have not [GOD], I am a noisy gong or a clanging cymbal. And if I have prophetic powers, and understand all mysteries and all knowledge, and if I have all faith, so as to remove mountains, but have not [GOD], I am nothing. If I give away all I have, and if I deliver up my body to be burned, but have not [GOD], I gain nothing."

God is the reason, God is the main event, God is the primary entity. Why? Because God is LOVE!

Questions to Ponder:

Am I ready to be an ambassador for Jesus?

Am I ready to be rejected, abused and alienated because I am now a member of God's family, not the world?

Do I have the love of God dwelling in me and am I willing to share that love with my fellow humans?

Take Away Notes:

BIBLIOGRAPHY

n.d. "2 Corinthians 5:18, Elliot's Commentary for English Readers." Accessed February 9, 2020. https://biblehub.com/commentaries/2_corinthians/5-18.htm.

Abbott, Shari. 2018. "What Does It Mean to Taste and See That God Is Good? (Psalm 34)." August 18. Accessed February 9, 2020. https://reasonsforhopejesus.com/taste-and-see/.

Adult Sabbath School Bible Study Guide. 2018. Fourth Quarter ed.: 16.

Adult Sabbath School Bible Study Guide. 2018. "Oneness in Christ." October–December: 47.

Albom, Mitch. 2009. *Have a Little Faith: A True Story.* New York, New York: Hyperion.

Andrews University Press. n.d. *Andrews University Bible.* Berrien Springs, Michigan: Andrews University Press.

Baker, L.S. Jr. 2009. "Covered with blood: A better understanding of Exodus 12:7." *Ministry Magazine*, September. Accessed February 9, 2020. https://www.ministrymagazine.org/archive/2009/09/covered-with-blood.html.

Biblehub. n.d. "John 12:32, Ellicott's Commentary for English Readers." Accessed February 9, 2020. https://biblehub.com/commentaries/john/12-32.htm.

Blake, Chris. 1991. *Searching for a God to Love.* Nampa, Ohio: Pacific Press Publishing.

Boutwell, Allison. 2015. "What Are God's Statutes?" February 19. Accessed February 9, 2020. https://allisonlboutwell.wordpress.com/2015/02/19/what-are-gods-statutes/.

Brown, Nathan. 2018. *For the Least of These*. Nampa, Idaho: Pacific Press.

Compelling Truth. n.d. "What is significant about the Ark of the Covenant? What is it?" Accessed February 9, 2020. https://www.compellingtruth.org/What-Ark-of-the-Covenant.html.

Easton, M.G. 1897. *Illustrated Bible Dictionary*. 3rd. Nashville, Tennessee: Thomas Nelson.

n.d. "Ephesians 2:16, Elliott's Commentary for English Readers." Accessed February 9, 2020. https://biblehub.com/commentaries/ephesians/2—16.htm.

n.d. "Exodus 3:16." Accessed February 9, 2020. https://www.bible-studytools.com/commentaries/gills-exposition-of-the-bible/exodus-32-16.html.

Finney, Charles G. 1861. "Hardness of Heart." March 16. Accessed February 9, 2020. https://www.gospeltruth.net/1861OE/610313_hardness_heart.htm.

Gibbs, Noni Beth. 2007. *Peter: Fisher of Men*. Oshawa, Ontario: Pacific Press Publishing Association.

Got Questions. n.d. "Why did God harden Pharaoh's heart?" Accessed February 9, 2020. https://www.gotquestions.org/God-harden-Pharaoh-heart.html.

Hardinge, Leslie. 2004. *Ambassadors: Studies on the 13 Apostles*. Hagerstown, Maryland: Review and Herald Publishing Association.

2001. "How did the Urim and the Thummim function?" January 1. Accessed February 9, 2020. https://bible.org/question/how-did-urim-and-thummim-function.

Husband, Darryl Sr. F. 2008. *The Altared Life: The Pathway Towards Revival*. Morrisville, North Carolina: Lulu Press.

Internet Archive. 2006. "A Biblical and theological dictionary." July

7. Accessed February 9, 2020. https://archive.org/details/abiblicalandtheo00unknuoft/page/n425/mode/2up.

n.d. "John 12:32, Ellicott's Commentary for English Readers." Accessed February 9, 2020. https://biblehub.com/commentaries/john/12-32.htm.

Klingbeil, Gerald A. 2019. "The Joy of the Lord Is Your Strength." *Adventist Journey*, June.

Lucado, Max. 1994. *When God Whispers Your Name.* Dallas, Texas: Word Publishing.

Mailman, The Orange. 2013. "Why did Moses break the stone tablets?" May 30. Accessed February 9, 2020. https://theorangemailmanmyblog.wordpress.com/2013/05/30/why-did-moses-break-the-stone-tablets/.

McCarty, Skip. 2007. *In Granite or Ingrained? What the Old and New Covenants Reveal about the Gospel, the Law, and the Sabbath.* Kindle. Berrien Springs, Michigan: Andrews University Press.

2010. "Moses: The First Commandment Breaker." May 10. Accessed February 9, 2020. https://www.thesimpleanswers.com/2010/05/10/moses-the-first-commandment-breaker/.

Paul, Mano. 2009. "It Is Finished—Genesis to Revelation." March 7. Accessed February 9, 2020. https://thepauls.wordpress.com/2009/03/07/it-is-finished-genesis-to-revelation/.

Snapp, Allen. 2017. "Setting Our Minds on Things Above." July 30. Accessed February 30, 2020. https://www.gracecorning.org/sermons/sermon/2017-07-30/setting-our-minds-on-things-above.

Seals, The Chief Engraver of Her Majesty's, ed. 2017. "The Great Seal in the reign of King George V." Vers. Public Domain. *Wikipedia.* Royal Archives. July 7. Accessed February 9, 2020. https://commons.wikimedia.org/wiki/File:Great_Seal_of_Canada_-_King_George_V.jpg.

White, Ellen G. 1941. *Christ's Object Lessons.* Rocky Hill, Connecticut: Review and Herald Publishing Association.

—. 1984. *From Trials to Triumph.* Oshawa, Ontario: Pacific Press Publishing Association.

—. 1946. *Patriarchs and Prophets.* Oshawa, Ontario: Signs of the Times Publishing Association.

—. 1943. *Prophets and Kings.* Nampa, Idaho: Pacific Press Publishing Association.

—. 1997. *Steps to Christ.* Nampa, Idaho: Pacific Press Publishing Association.

—. 1911. *The Acts of the Apostles.* Mountain View, California: Pacific Press Publishing Association.

—. 2005. *The Desire of Ages.* Oshawa, Ontario: Pacific Press Publishing Association.

—. 1950. *The Great Controversy Between Christ and Satan.* Oshawa, Ontario: Pacific Press Publishing Association.

—. 1942. *The Ministry of Healing.* Oshanawa, Ontario: Pacific Press Publishing Association.

—. 1955. *The Mount of Blessings.* (Oshawa, Ontario: Pacific Press Publishing Association.

n.d. *Who were the Canaanites?* Accessed February 9, 2020. https://www.gotquestions.org/Canaanites.html.

Williams, Hyveth. 2004. *Secrets of a Happy Heart: A Fresh Look at the Sermon on the Mount.* (Hagerstown, Maryland: Review and Herald Publishing Association.

CPSIA information can be obtained
at www.ICGtesting.com
Printed in the USA
LVHW031645040121
675584LV00029B/653

9 781949 758832